Collins
Assessment

Assessing Receptive Vocabulary

Age 6–7

Clare Dowdall

William Collins' dream of knowledge for all began with the publication of his first book in 1819. A self-educated mill worker, he not only enriched millions of lives, but also founded a flourishing publishing house. Today, staying true to this spirit, Collins books are packed with inspiration, innovation and practical expertise. They place you at the centre of a world of possibility and give you exactly what you need to explore it.

Collins. Freedom to teach.

Collins
An imprint of HarperCollins*Publishers*
The News Building
1 London Bridge Street
London
SE1 9GF

Browse the complete Collins catalogue at **www.collins.co.uk**

© HarperCollins*Publishers* Limited 2018

10 9 8 7 6 5 4 3 2 1

ISBN 978-0-00-831149-0

British Library Cataloguing in Publication Data. A catalogue record for this publication is available from the British Library.

Author: Clare Dowdall
Publisher: Katie Sergeant
Senior Editor: Mike Appleton
Copyeditor: Tanya Solomons
Proofreader: Catherine Dakin
Cover designers: The Big Mountain Design, Ken Vail Graphic Design
Production controller: Katharine Willard
Printed and bound by CPI Group (UK) Ltd, Croydon, CR0 4YY

Contents

		Page
Introduction		4
Vocabulary lists		
1	Human body	7
2	Actions	9
3	More actions	11
4	Sports	13
5	Games	15
6	Animal parts	17
7	Animal life cycles	19
8	Growing a plant	21
9	Garden tools	23
10	At the farm	25
11	Wild animals	27
12	Creatures that sting or bite	29
13	At the seashore	31
14	In the rainforest	33
15	On the water	35
16	On the cycle path	37
17	At school and at work	39
18	At the campsite	41
19	At the concert	43
20	At the wedding	45
21	In the toolshed	47
22	Disasters	49
23	Vegetables	51
24	Healthy eating	53
25	Properties of materials	55
26	Continents and oceans	57
27	Around the globe	61
28	Landmarks	63
29	Life on earth	65
30	Habitats	67
Half termly test 1		69
Half termly test 2		84
Half termly test 3		99
Half termly test 4		114
Half termly test 5		129
Half termly test 6		144
Template to create own tests		159
Half termly tests teacher scripts		160
Half termly tests record sheets		163

How to use this book

Introduction

Collins Receptive Vocabulary lists and tests are designed to enhance and assess children's understanding of some of the key vocabulary that they may encounter as they progress through the early years of their education. The resource has been developed for use in Year 2/P3. It aims to provide teachers with a series of word lists and receptive vocabulary tests that are relevant to children's lives and the curriculum expectations for each stage of their learning.

What is receptive vocabulary?

Receptive vocabulary is a term used by educators, speech and language therapists and linguists (among others) to describe the set of words that an individual can understand when listening or reading. Receptive vocabulary is sometimes used alongside the term productive, or expressive, vocabulary, which describes the words that an individual can use when speaking or writing. For most people, their productive vocabulary includes well-known, familiar words that are used often. The receptive vocabulary may include less familiar words and is likely to be much more extensive than the productive vocabulary.

Why receptive vocabulary matters

The current national plan for social mobility through education in England, *Unlocking Talent, Fulfilling Potential* (DfE, 2017) states a clear ambition to close the reported 'word gap' in the early years of education. In this plan, a correlation between social disadvantage and slower rates of development in some children's early language and literacy is claimed. This deficit in language and literacy is described as a 'word gap'; a term that was coined in a seminal study conducted in the US over 20 years ago (see Hart and Risley: The Early Catastrophe. The 30 Million Word Gap). In a summary of their study, the authors claim that children from less advantaged backgrounds are exposed to dramatically less language than their more advantaged peers by the age of three, leading to lower educational attainment.

While this study and the use of its findings have been subject to considerable recent criticism relating to method and relevance (summarised by Kuchirko, 2017), it is currently regarded by policy makers in England as significant. Notably, the claims made in Hart and Risley's report feed into the larger claim: that the reported early literacy and language deficit – or word gap – can be actively tackled to support positive social mobility.

How can receptive vocabulary be developed?

Children's receptive vocabulary develops throughout childhood in the social, cultural and educational settings that children inhabit. Parents and carers are widely recognised in policy and research as being the child's first educators, and their role in early vocabulary development must be acknowledged. Children's receptive vocabulary can be further developed and extended by teachers using contextualised, meaningful experiences that involve speaking and listening in a variety of contexts and relating to a variety of topics. These will include child-initiated and practitioner-led play and learning activities in the classroom and beyond. In addition, immersing children in story worlds and rich, reading, talking and listening activities, such as shared and guided reading, and drama, are recognised as key strategies for expanding children's receptive vocabulary, and introducing them to new and varied language patterns and genres.

Alongside these everyday classroom practices, the use of a targeted vocabulary resource can support specific language development, and its assessment, and ensure that children's experience and development of a rich and varied vocabulary is maximised. This is the case for all children – but may be especially useful where teachers perceive that children have gaps in their receptive vocabulary. For example, children who have English as an additional language may appear proficient in their understanding and use of everyday language, but need further support when new topics are introduced to encounter and understand new topic-related words. This may also be the case for children where there is a perceived deficit in their receptive vocabulary, or evidence of a 'word-gap'.

How to use this book

Teachers often automatically support vocabulary development by facilitating talk-based pedagogies and activities that draw on children's own interests. Children's understanding and use of everyday vocabulary will develop in relation to these experiences. This responsive way of working will help familiar vocabulary to be used and consolidated within the child's lexicon.

In addition to this, the classroom setting provides an ideal environment for expanding children's interests to introduce them to new topics and their associated language. This is a key opportunity for enriching children's receptive vocabulary as they encounter new topic-based words and concepts. This more challenging and less familiar vocabulary will vary from setting to setting and child to child, but should reflect the child's needs, their developing awareness of the world around them, and relevant curriculum expectations and requirements.

Statutory requirements for spoken language within the English National Curriculum require all children to use relevant strategies to build their vocabulary (DFE, 2013). Requirements for Literacy and English within the Curriculum for Excellence require all children to extend and enrich their vocabulary through talking, listening, watching and reading (Education Scotland, 2018).

Teachers can be supported to expand children's exposure to new and unfamiliar vocabulary through using word lists that relate to curriculum areas and expectations, and resources to support the assessment of a child's developing receptive vocabulary.

About this book

The book is divided into two main sections. First, 30 topic-related receptive vocabulary lists are provided that can be used as stand-alone resources or to support topic teaching. These are followed by six half termly tests that can be used to support teachers' assessments of the extent of children's developing receptive vocabulary.

Word lists

The Collins Receptive Vocabulary lists are designed to support children's opportunities to encounter key topic-related vocabulary, and for teachers to be able to develop and assess children's receptive vocabulary as drawn from these topic areas. In particular, the vocabulary lists can be used as the basis for creating a range of resources and activities, including displays, flash cards and matching games, as well as assessing children's receptive vocabulary in relation to the topic.

The resource is presented as a series of 30 topic-related word lists for each year group. Each word list contains 10 words, presented using simple line-drawn illustrations. Each list has a topic heading that indicates how the vocabulary contained within it might connect to children's lives and learning experiences. Topics for each year group have been selected to include links to the key relevant curriculum areas, popular areas of study, and children's interests and experiences. As such, the word lists aim to include the key vocabulary that children might encounter or need to understand, in educational settings and at home, as their lexicon grows.

The 30 topic-related word lists for each year group are designed to be used in any order. This will allow teachers to plan in a responsive way, and make connections to children's interests and teaching priorities. The topics that may be more familiar to children appear first in each list; the less familiar topics follow. In this way, a sense of progression can be implied through the resource, although this will depend on the experiences of the children in each situation.

Each word list includes 10 words. These are listed for the teacher and presented as illustrations for use when developing children's receptive vocabulary. The words included in each topic list are usually nouns. This means that the resource can be used to support explicit grammatical awareness, in addition to enhancing children's receptive vocabulary in each topic area.

It is envisaged that these lists may support teachers to produce displays of key vocabulary, and to check the range of vocabulary that children are exposed to as they plan for each topic area.

How to use this book

Tests

The 30 word lists are followed by six tests that can be used to establish the extent of children's receptive vocabulary at half termly intervals throughout the year. Each test assesses children's understanding of 15 words that have been selected from across the topic lists for the whole year.

Each 'test' word is presented using an illustration from the topic word list, alongside three other illustrations from the same list, on a single sheet. This means that the test can be used to assess knowledge of the 'test' word, or of any of the surrounding words from the topic.

To assess receptive vocabulary, teachers are prompted to proceed in the following way:

Teacher prompt:
Can you tell me which one shows ...? Or
Can you show me the ...?

The test is designed to assess children's receptive vocabulary in relation to the word lists contained in this resource. This means that the teacher is looking for the child's ability to **understand the word being said to them and identify it using an illustration**. The child can simply point to the illustration or may wish to talk about it.

Teachers may choose to take the opportunity to ask about the other illustrations, and this will be a useful opportunity to assess children's wider use of vocabulary in relation to this topic area.

A separate sheet is provided for teachers to record whether children can identify the test word in each set of words.

If the child can identify the correct illustration for the word given, the box should be ticked.

If the child is unable to identify the correct illustration for the word given, the box should be left blank.

At the end of each test, the child will have a score out of 15.

The test results can be used to identify strengths and gaps in individual children's receptive vocabulary in relation to specific topic areas and across a range of topics. In addition, the assessment information can be used to compare the child's receptive vocabulary to their peers who have had similar exposure to topic-related vocabulary in the classroom. This comparison may help to identify children who will benefit from targeted vocabulary work. Equally, the information may be used to identify children with strong receptive vocabulary whose language work may be open to further extension.

References

Department for Education (DfE) (2017) *Unlocking talent, Fulfilling Potential* [online] available at https://www.gov.uk/government/publications/improving-social-mobility-through-education (accessed June 18, 2018)

Hart, B. and Risley, T.R. (2003) The Early Catastrophe. The 30 Million Word Gap in *American Educator*, Volume 27 no.1 pp 4–9

Kuchirko, Y. (2017) On differences and deficits: A critique of the theoretical and methodological underpinnings of the word gap, in *Journal of Early Childhood Literacy* [online first] available at http://journals.sagepub.com/doi/full/10.1177/1468798417747029 (accessed June 18, 2018)

Hiebert, E.H. and Kamil, M.L. (2005) *Teaching and Learning Vocabulary: Bringing Research to Practice*, Lawrence Erlbaum and Associates Inc.: New Jersey

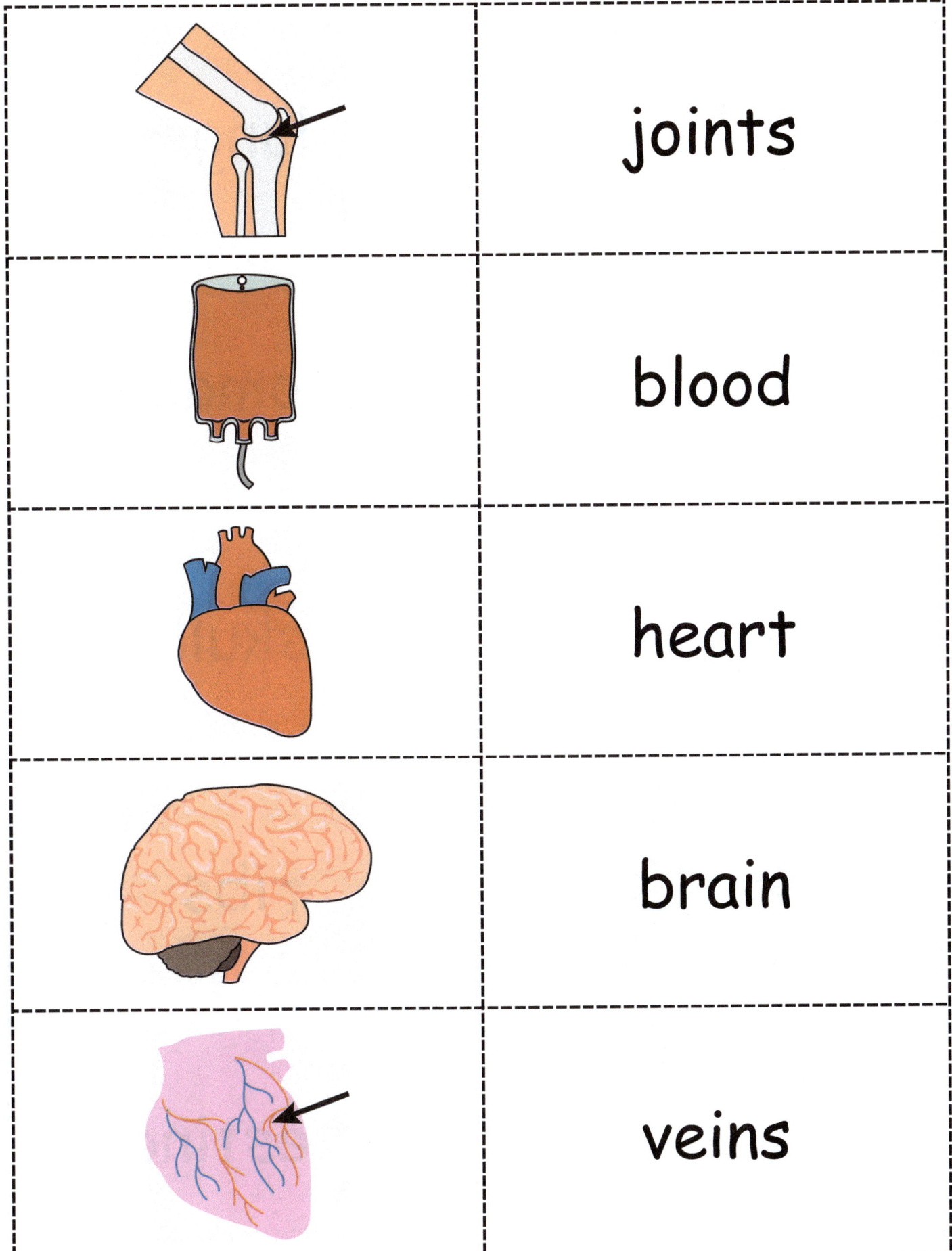

	joints
	blood
	heart
	brain
	veins

	lungs
	stomach
	skull
	ribs
	intestines

	cutting
	sewing
	pointing
	swimming
	cooking

Class _____

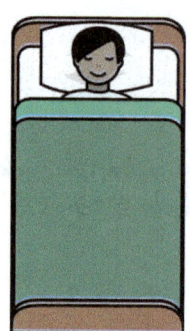

sleeping

running

hopping

singing

reading

	dancing
	digging
	chopping
	balancing
	writing

Class _____

	fighting
	skipping
	climbing
	stretching
	throwing

Class _____

	tennis
	swimming
	football
	cricket
	rugby

Class _____

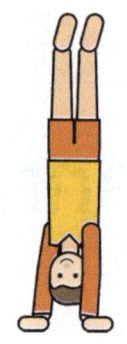	gymnastics
	running
	basketball
	cycling
	karate

Class _____

	playing cards
	dominoes
	skittles
 	tag
	marbles

Games

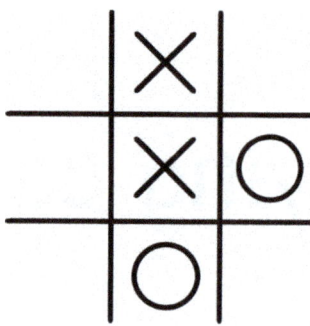	**noughts and crosses**
	**dice**
	**chess**
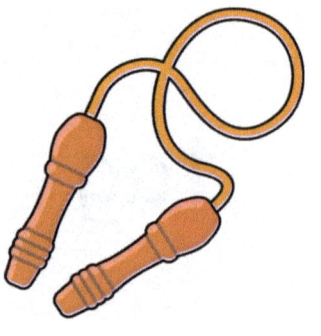	**skipping**
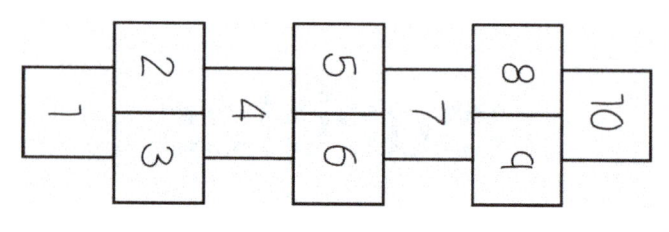	**hopscotch**

	whiskers
	paw
	claw
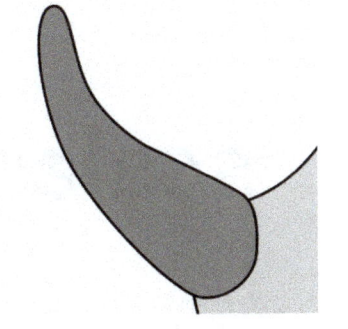	flipper
	horn

Class _____

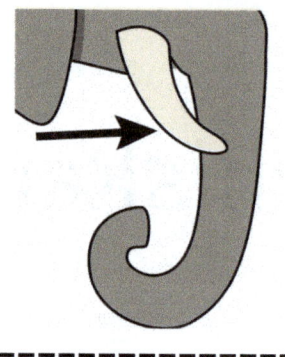	tusk
	mane
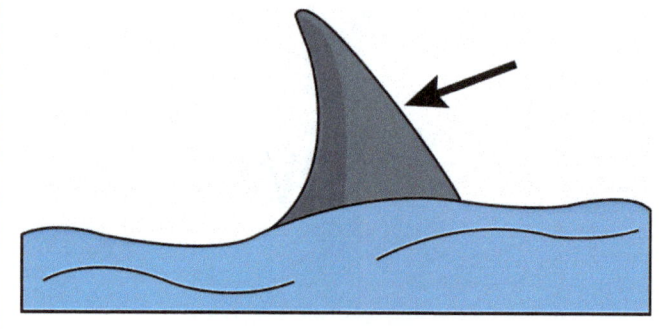	fin
	feather
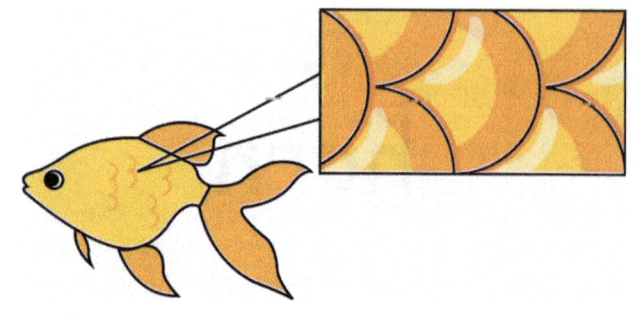	scales

 Animal parts

Class _____

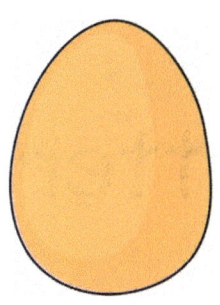	egg
	chick
	chicken
	caterpillar
	pupa

Animal life cycles

Class _____

	butterfly
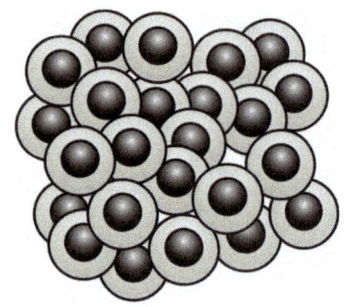	frogspawn
	tadpoles
	frog
	life cycle

Animal life cycles

Class _____

	seeds
	bulb
	fruit
	water
	sunlight

 Growing a plant

Class _____

	soil
	bud
	shade
	flower
	compost

Growing a plant

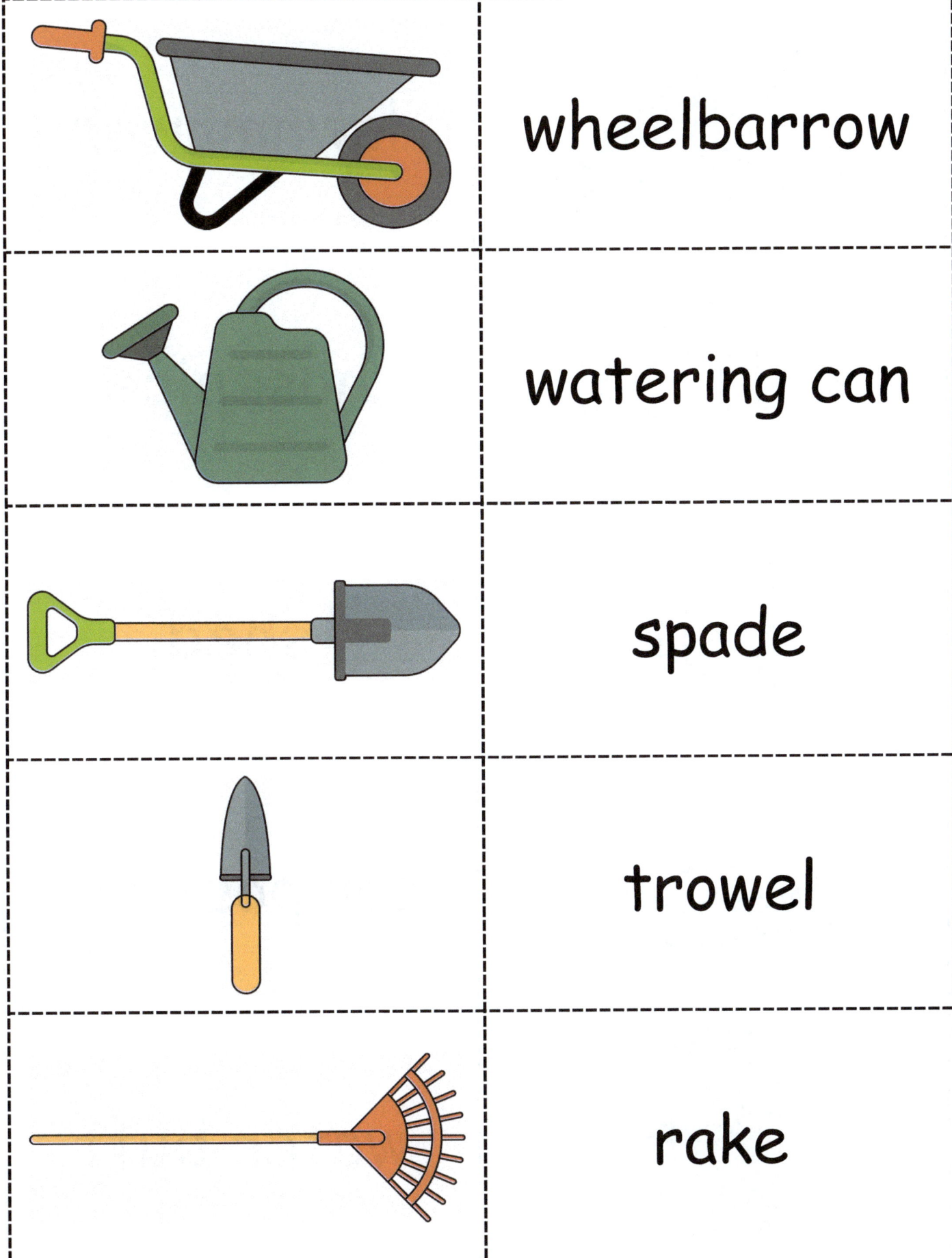

	wheelbarrow
	watering can
	spade
	trowel
	rake

Class _____

	lawnmower
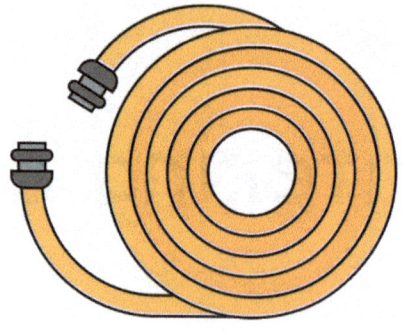	hosepipe
	shed
	compost bin
	water butt

Garden tools

	cowshed
	stable
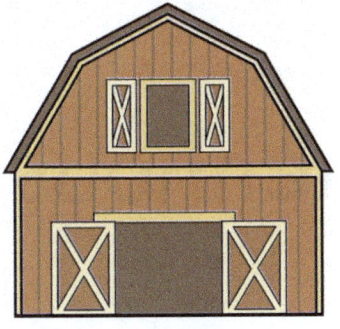	barn
	farmhouse
	duck pond

	orchard
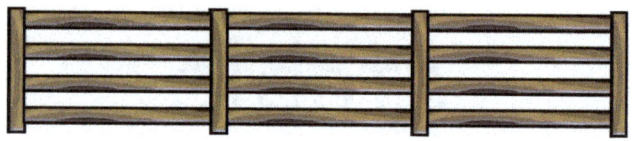	fence
	henhouse
	farmyard
	haystack

	panda
	dolphin
	gorilla
	ostrich
	kangaroo

Class _____

bear

camel

cheetah

anteater

porcupine

Wild animals

Class _____

	spider
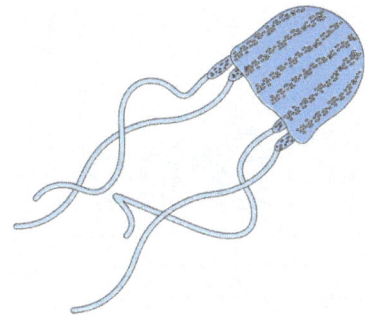	jellyfish
	snake
	crocodile
	shark

Creatures that sting or bite

Class _____

	mosquito
	frog
	octopus
	wasp
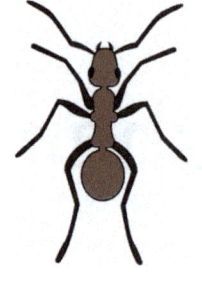	ant

     Creatures that sting or bite

Class _____

	rock pool
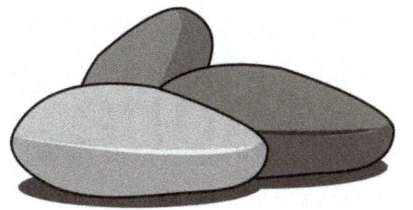	pebbles
	waves
	hermit crab
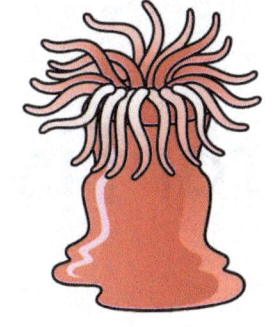	anemone

At the seashore

Class _____

	cliffs
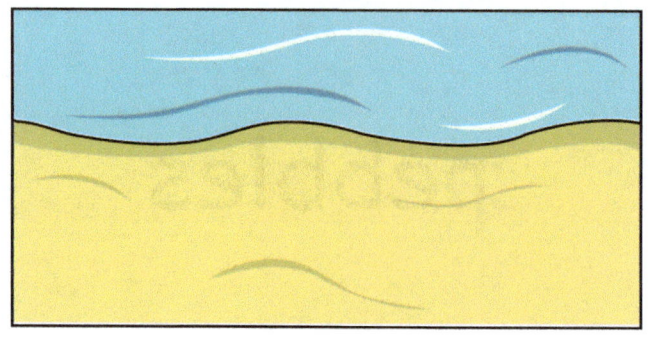	shore
	seaweed
	limpet
	starfish

 At the seashore

Class _____

	toucan
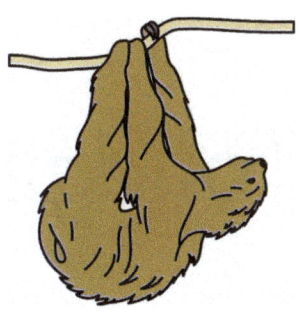	sloth
	bat
	leopard
	waterfall

In the rainforest

	**forest floor**
	**foliage**
	**canopy**
	**understory**
	**vines**

Class _____

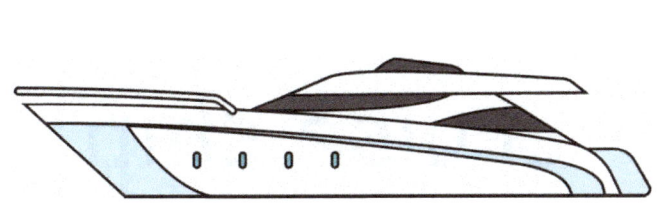	yacht
	water skis
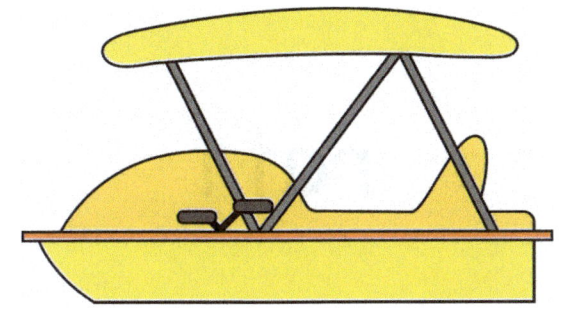	pedalo
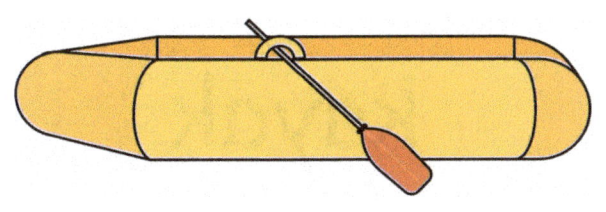	dinghy
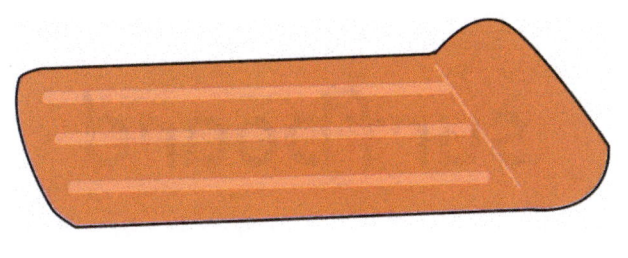	lilo

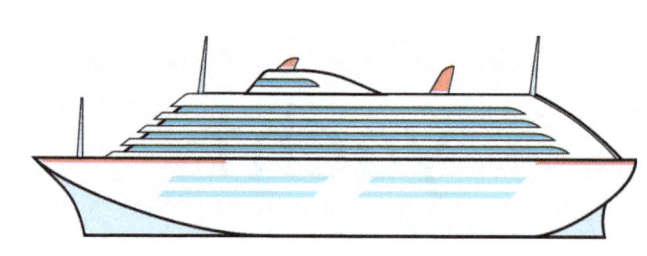

cruise ship

speedboat

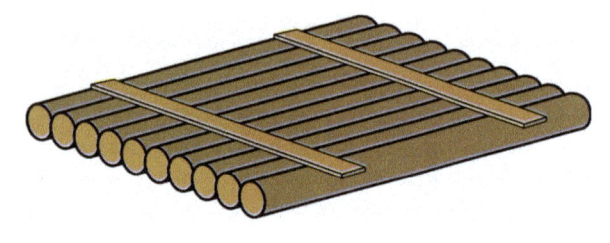

raft

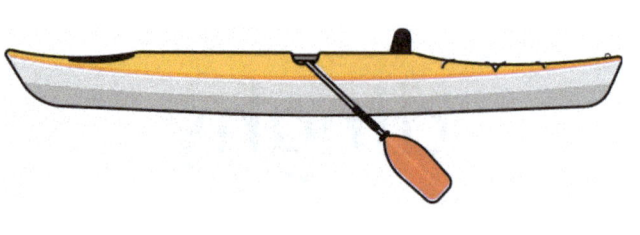

kayak

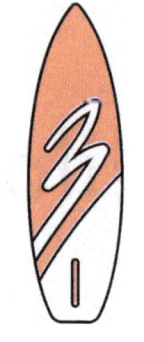

surfboard

     On the water

Class _____

	bicycle
	chain
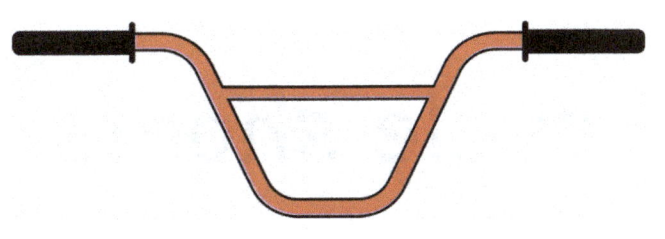	handlebars
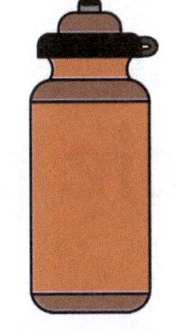	water bottle
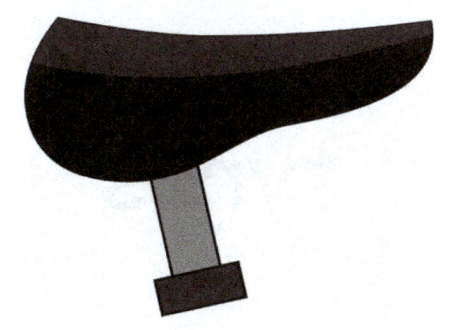	saddle

On the cycle path

Class _____

	saddlebag
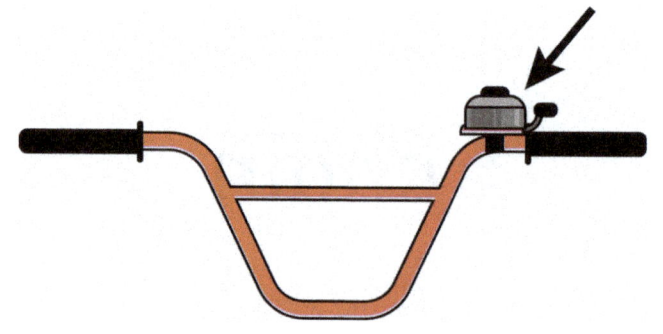	bell
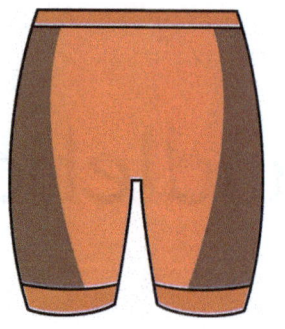	cycle shorts
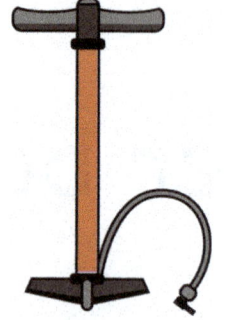	bicycle pump
	tyres

On the cycle path

Class _____

	desk
	computer
	briefcase
	lunchbox
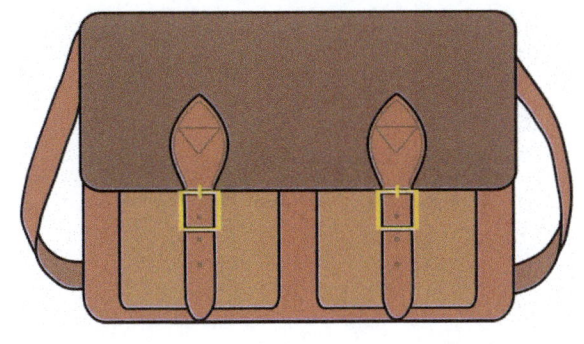	school bag

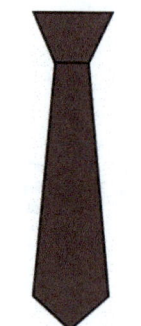	tie
	blazer
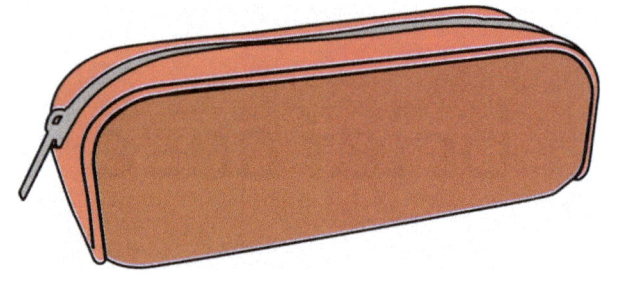	pencil case
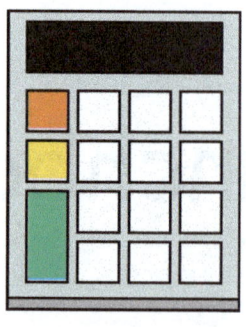	calculator
	notebook

     At school and at work

	tent
	camp bed
	sleeping bag
	pillow
	trailer

Class _____

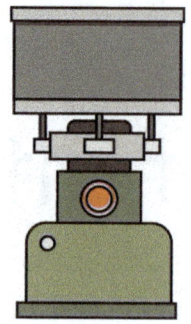	**camping stove**
	**camp fire**
	**roll mat**
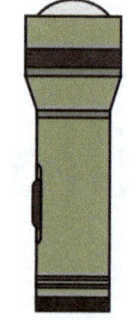	**torch**
	**penknife**

	orchestra
	music stand
	conductor
	instruments
	drummer

Class _____

	sheet music
	audience
	popstar
	stage
	microphone

	bride
	groom
	bridesmaid
	pageboy
	posy

	veil
	confetti
	photographer
	cake
	rings

	axe
	saw
	hammer
	spanner
	tape measure

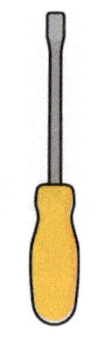	screwdriver
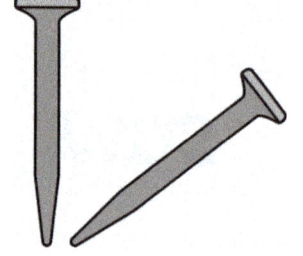	nails
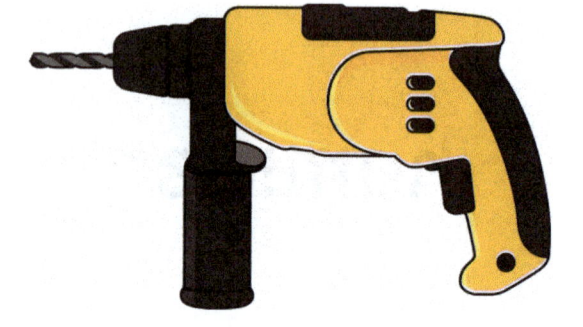	drill
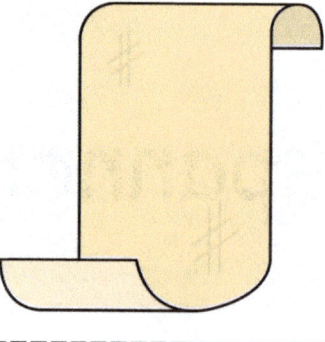	sandpaper
	ladder

In the toolshed

Class _____

	earthquake
	volcano
	hurricane
	tsunami
	forest fire

   Disasters

flood

tornado

snowstorm

avalanche

landslide

Disasters

	**Brussels sprouts**
	cabbage
	cauliflower
	courgette
	aubergine

© HarperCollins*Publishers* Ltd 2018

Vegetables

Class _____

sugar snap

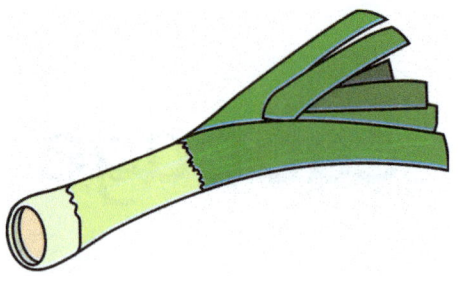

leek

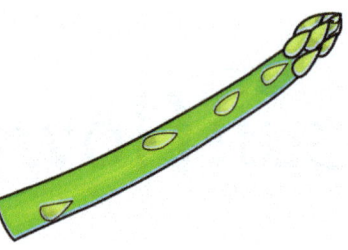

asparagus

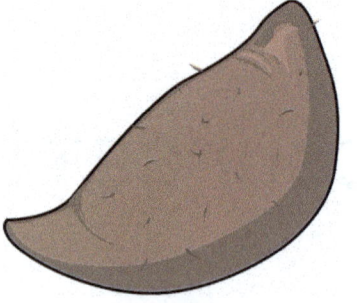

sweet potato

pumpkin

 Vegetables

Class _____

	fruit
	vegetables
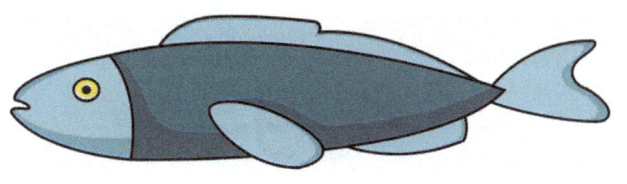	fish
	meat
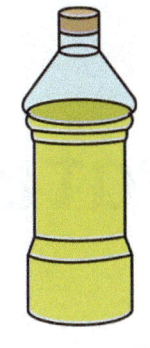	oil

Class _____

	beans
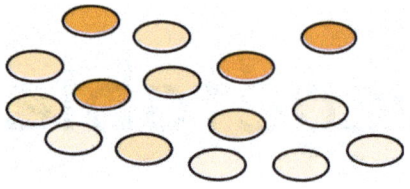	lentils
	eggs
	cheese
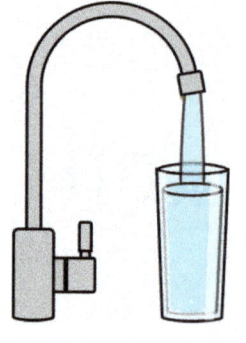	water

 Healthy eating

Class _____

	waterproof
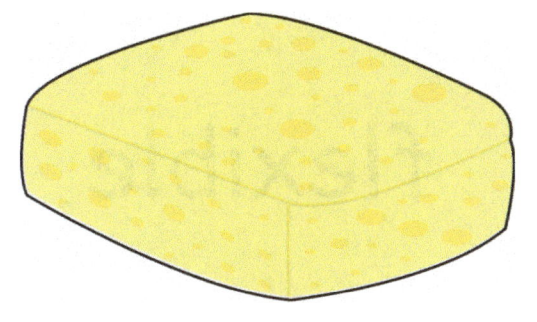	porous
	absorbent
	opaque
	transparent

Class _____

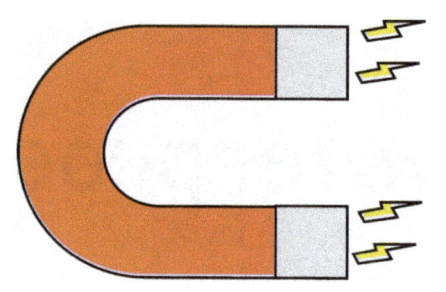	magnetic
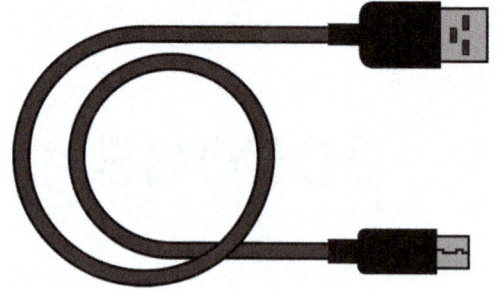	flexible
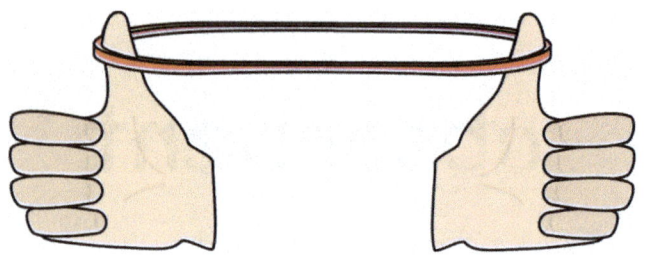	stretchy
	brittle
	flammable

Properties of materials

North America

South America

Europe

Continents and oceans

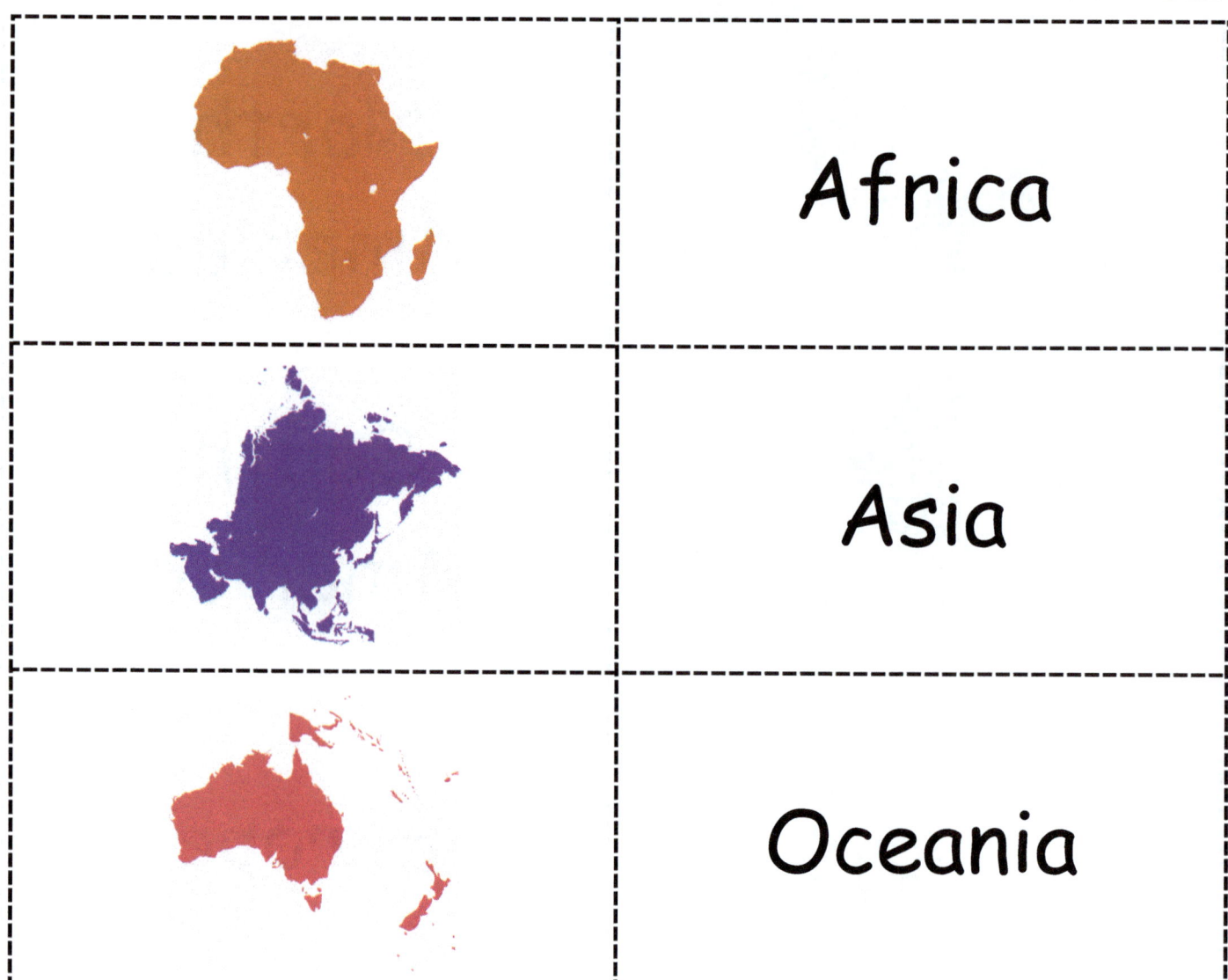

	Africa
	Asia
	Oceania

Continents and oceans

Class _____

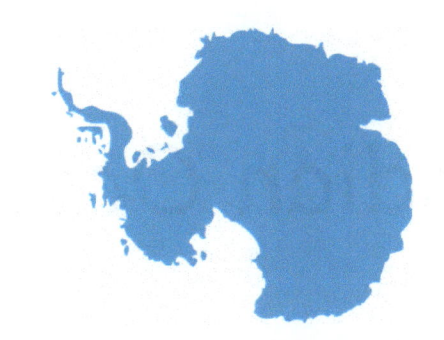	Antarctica
	Pacific Ocean
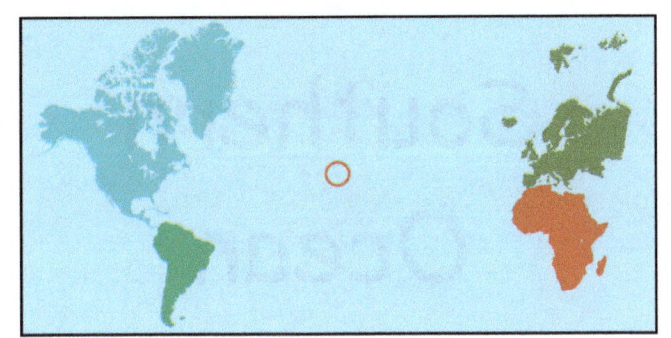	Atlantic Ocean

 Continents and oceans

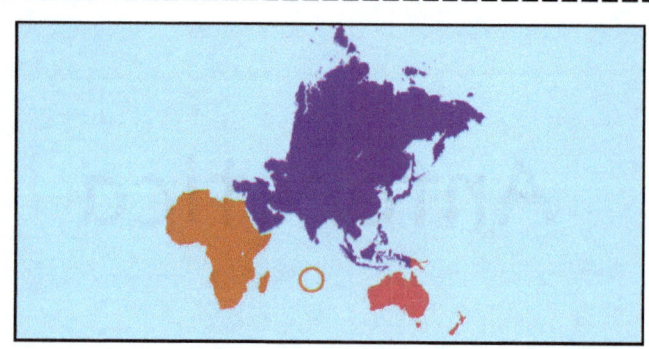

Indian Ocean

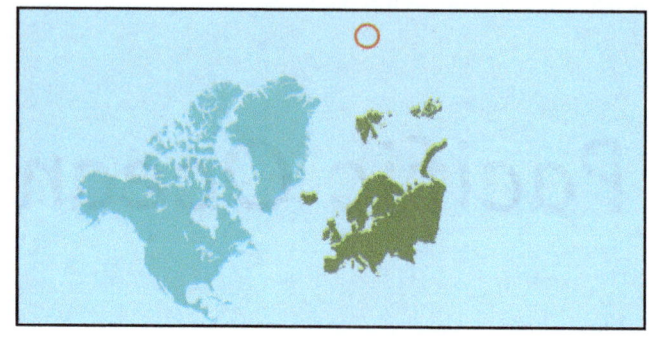

Arctic Ocean

Southern Ocean

	Equator
	North Pole
	South Pole
	North
	East

Class _____

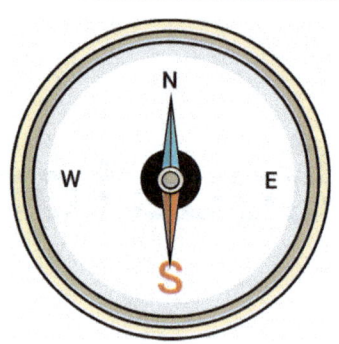	South
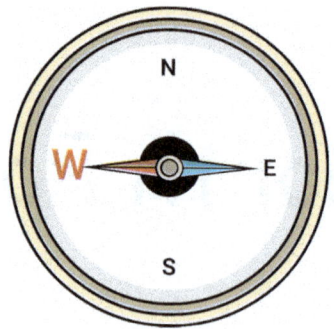	West
	globe
	atlas
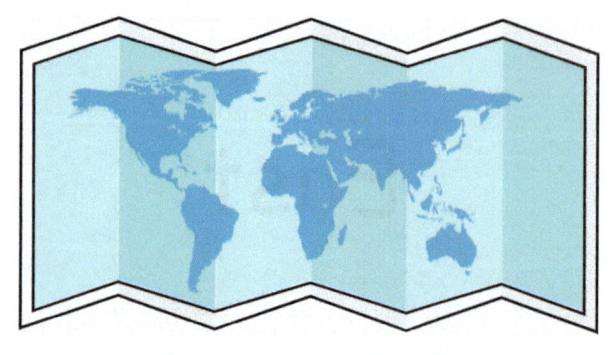	map

Class _____

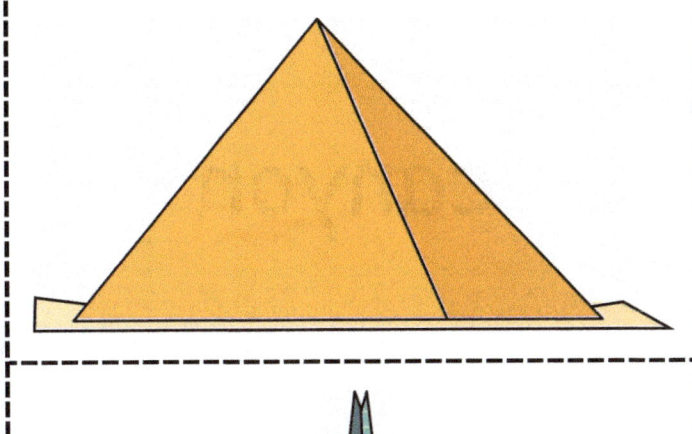	pyramid
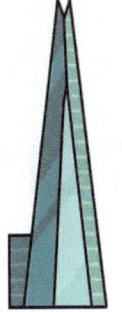	skyscraper
	palace
	wall
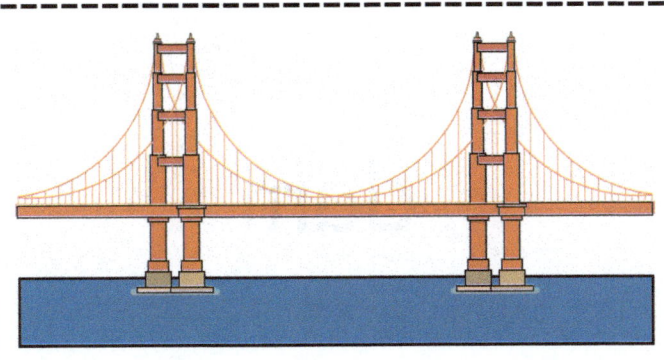	bridge

Class _____

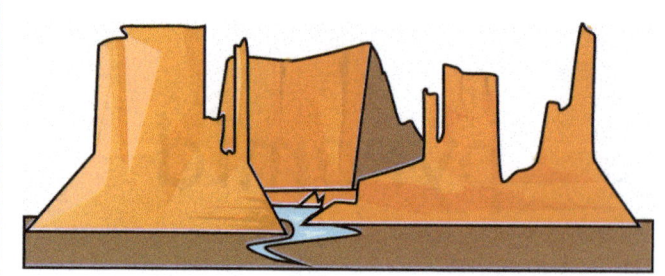	canyon
	waterfall
	mosque
	cathedral
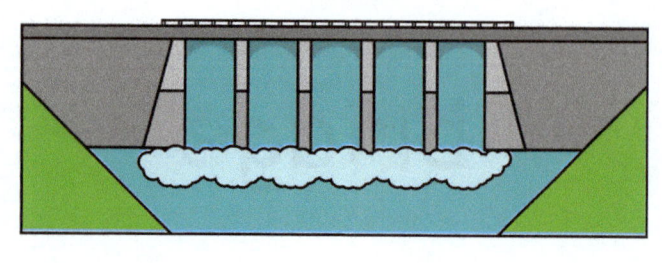	dam

	carnivore
	mammals
	birds
	reptiles
	amphibians

Class _____

	fish
	herbivore
	arthropods
	insects
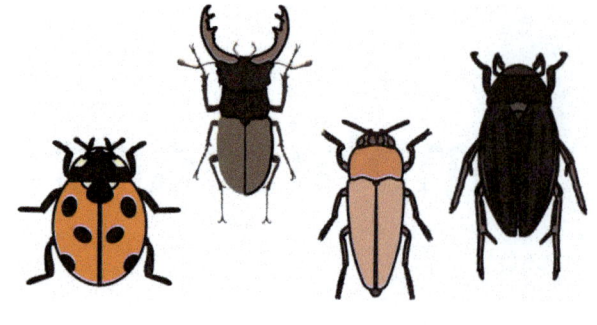	beetles

       Life on earth

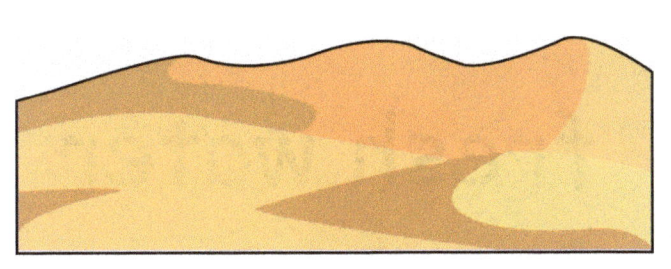	desert
	grasslands
	forest
	mountains
	polar regions

Class _____

	**fresh water**
	**wetland**
	**ocean**
	**coral reef**
	**swamp**

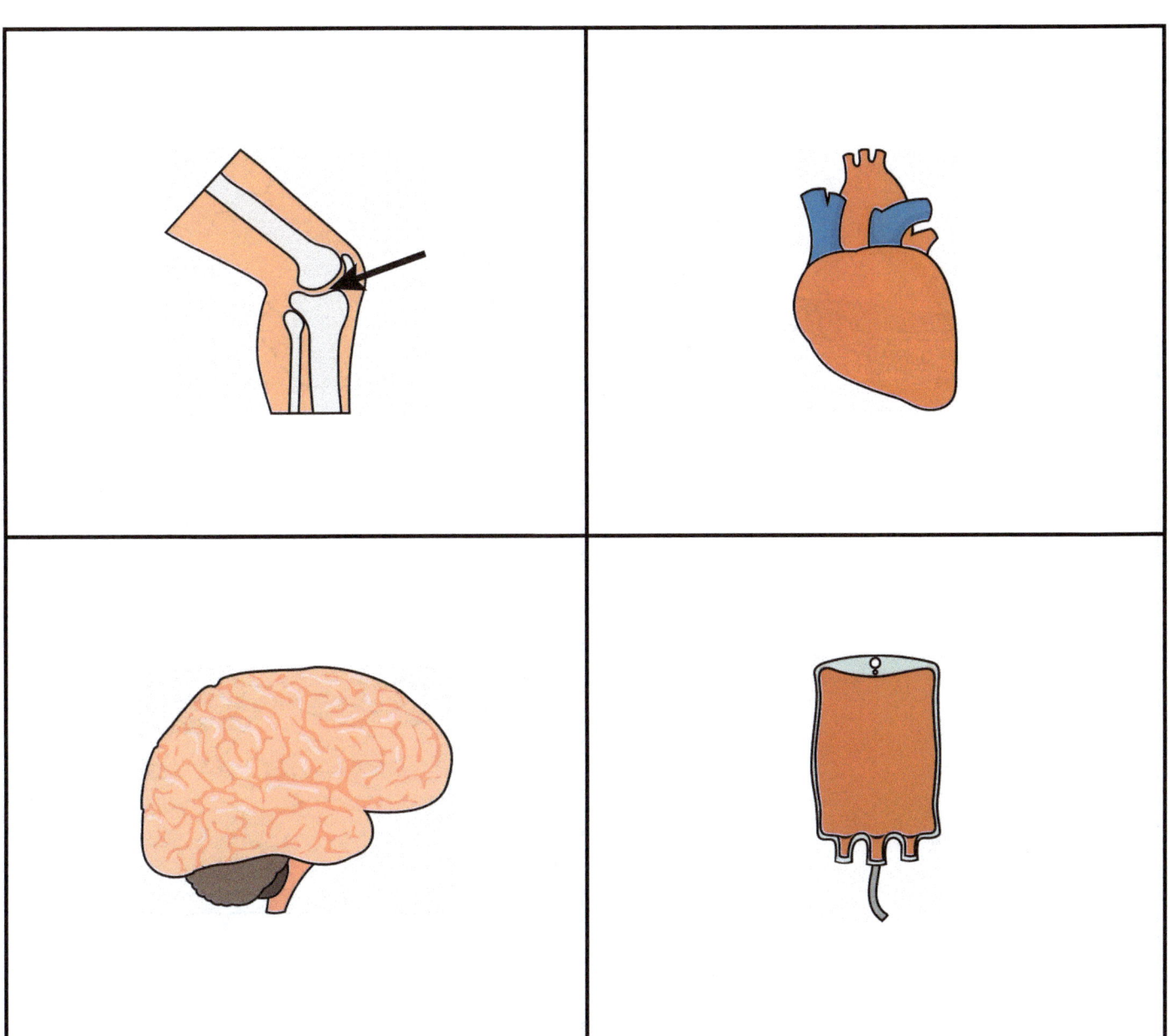

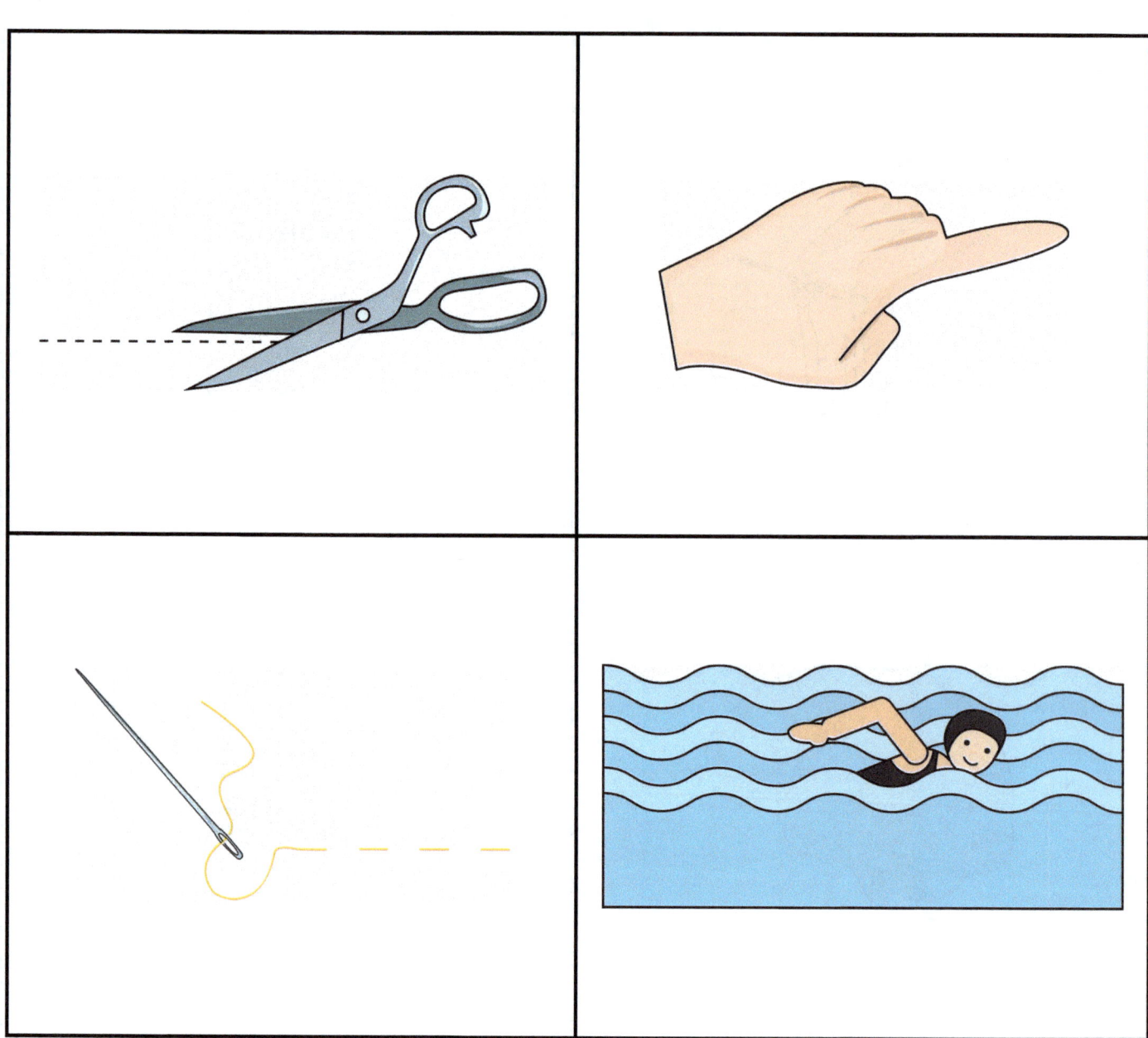

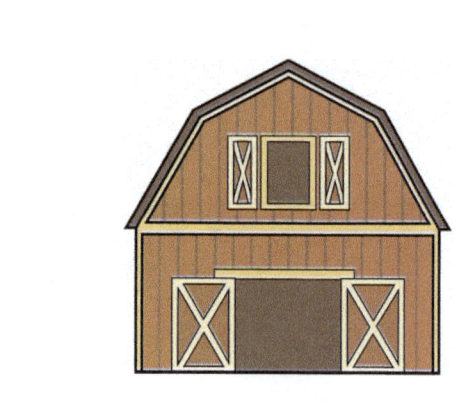

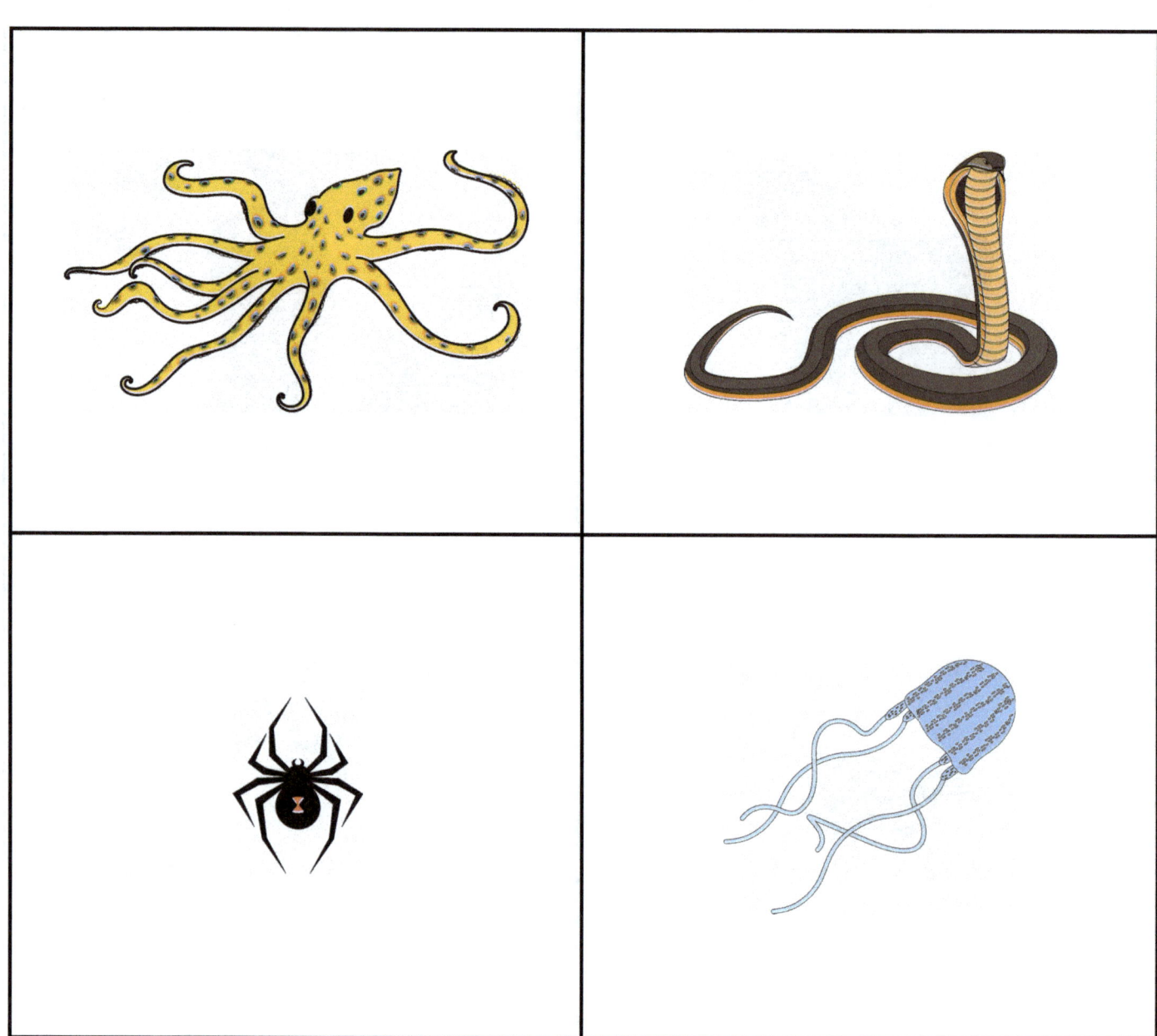

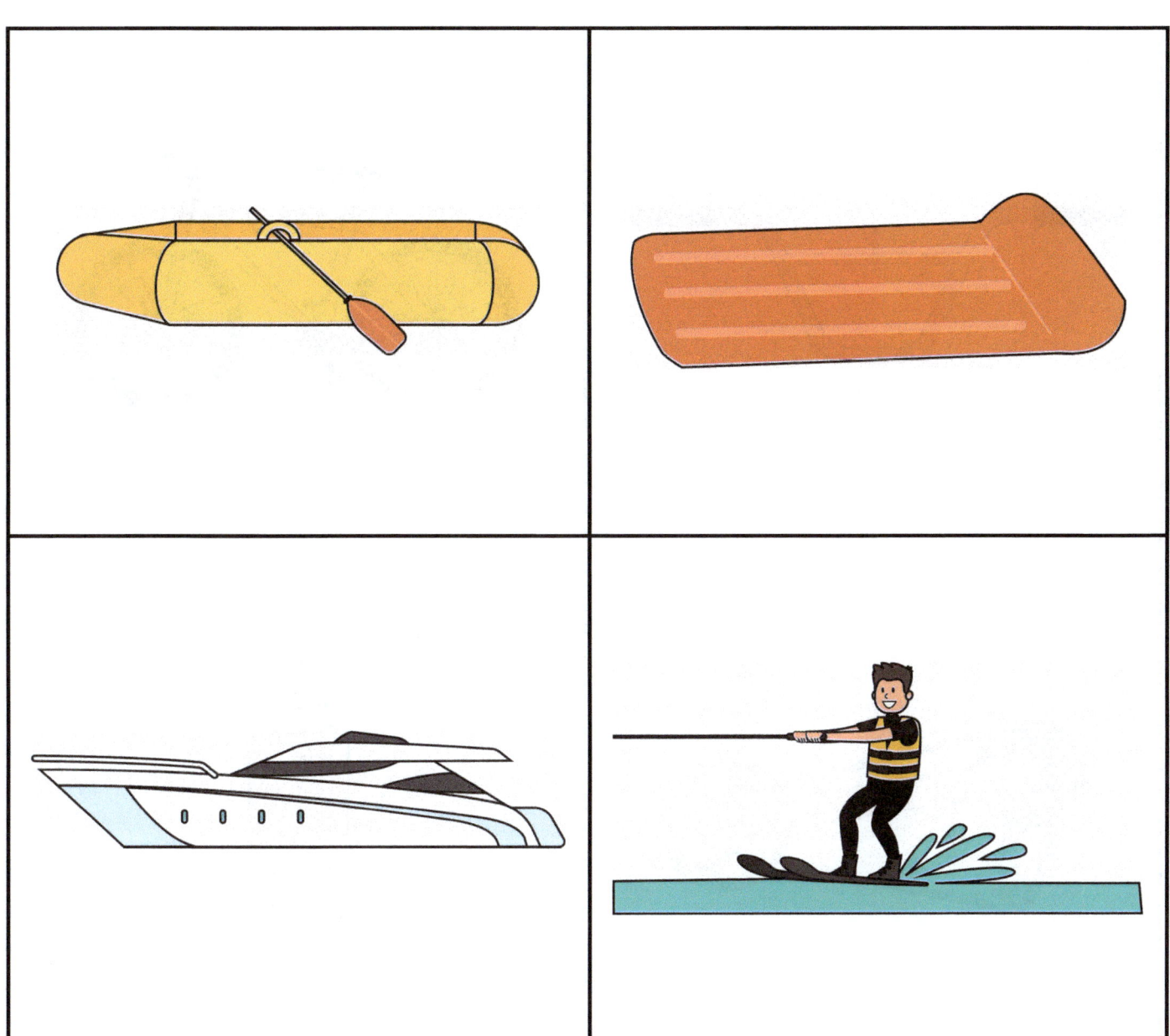

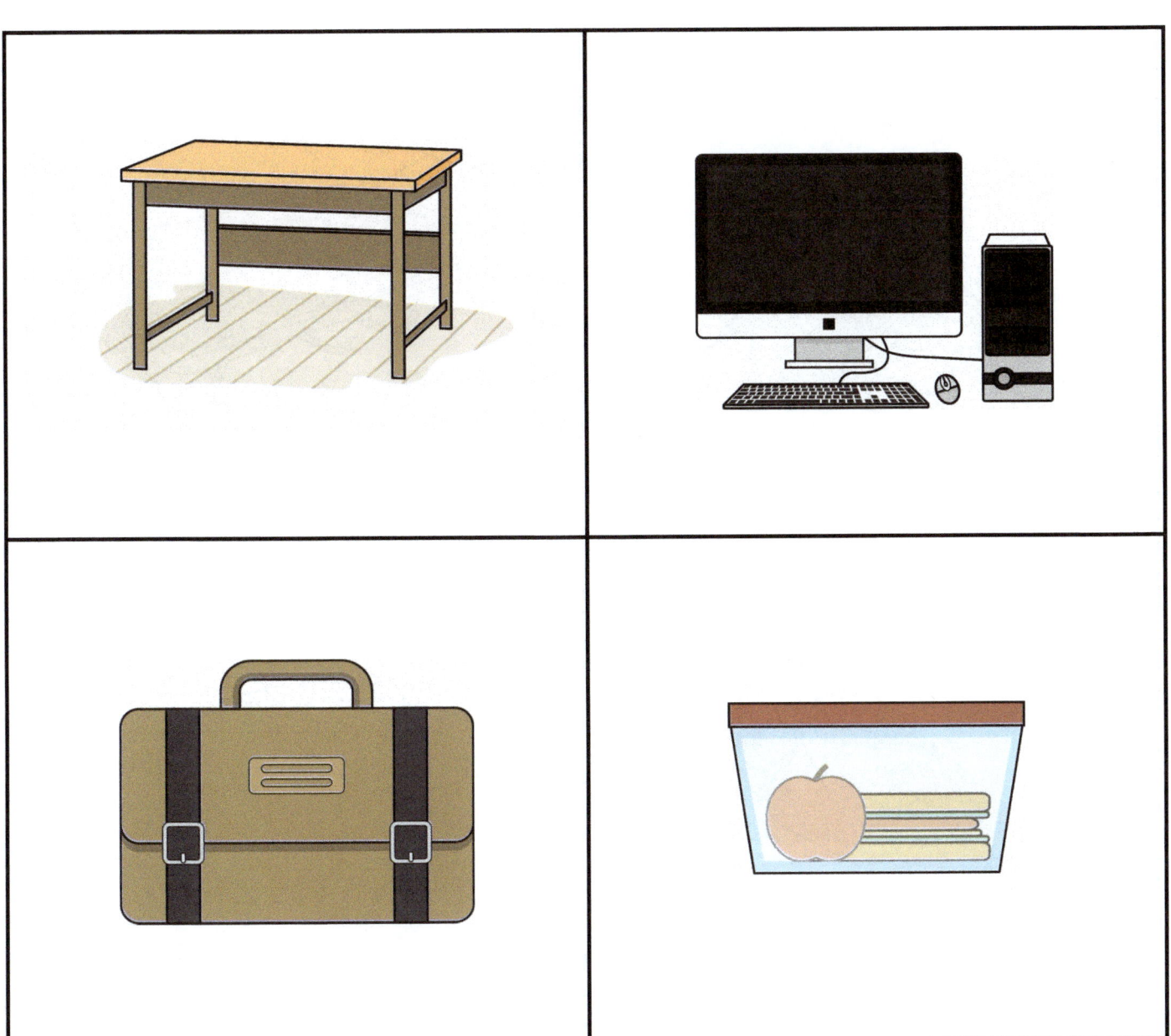

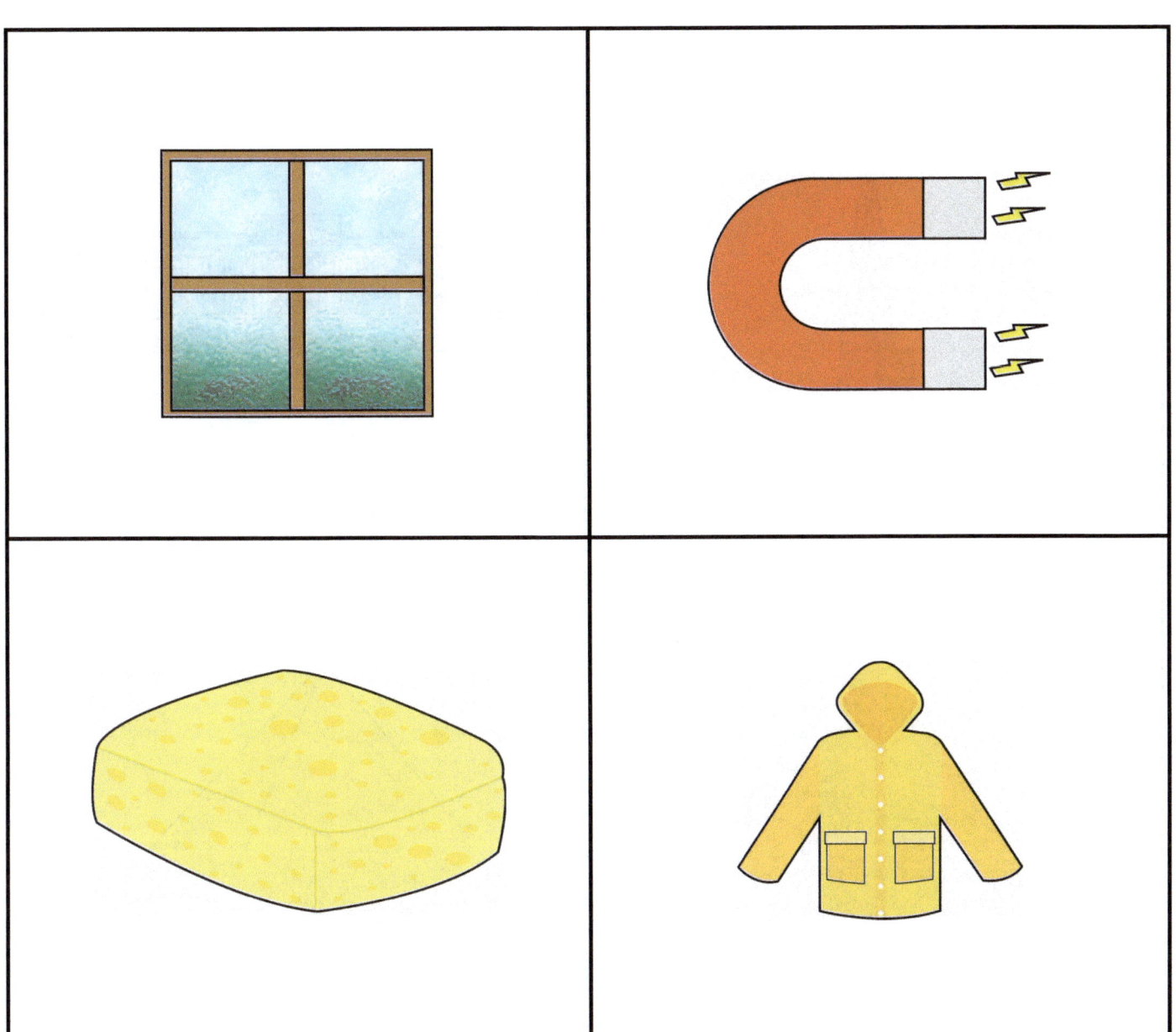

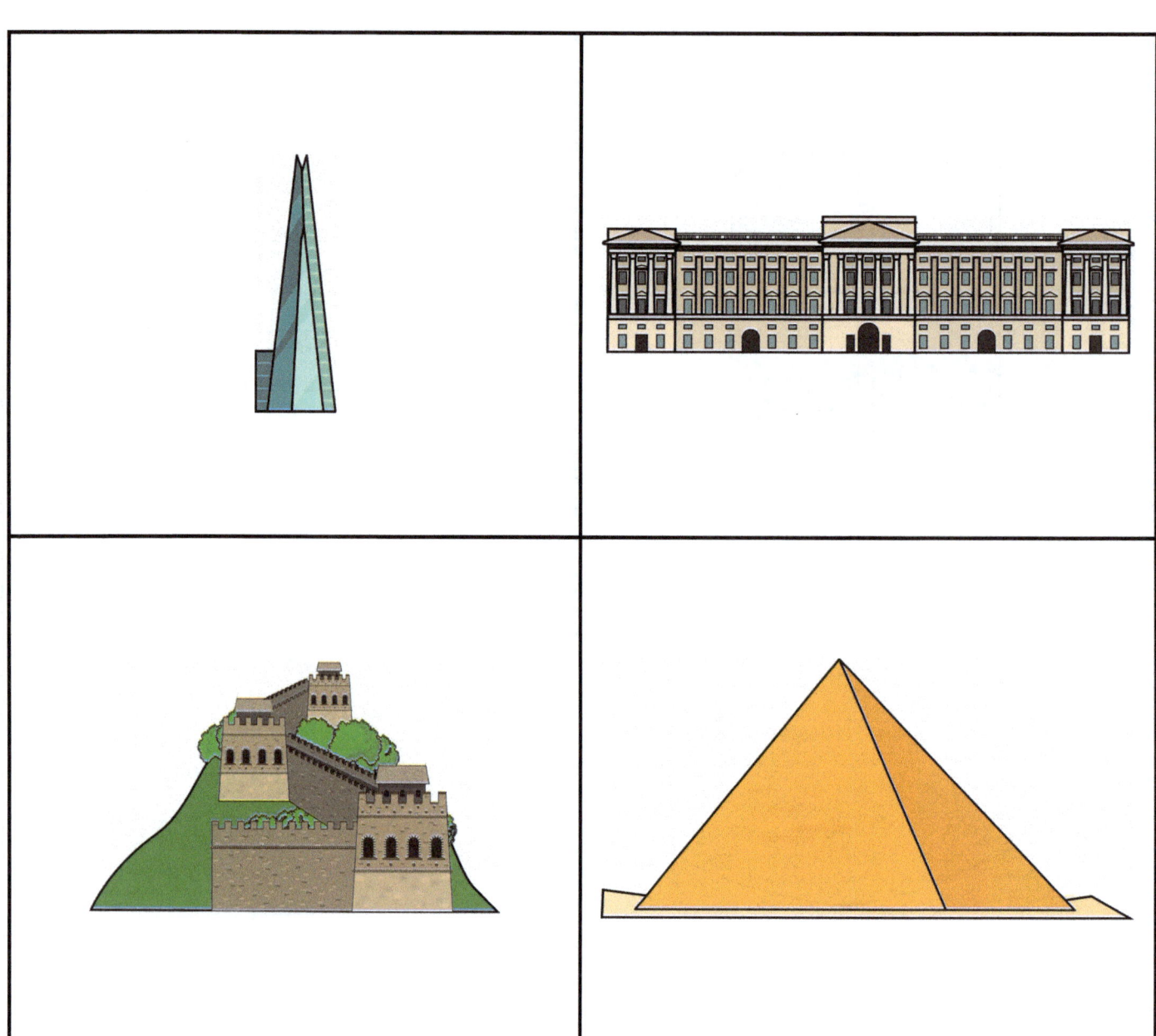

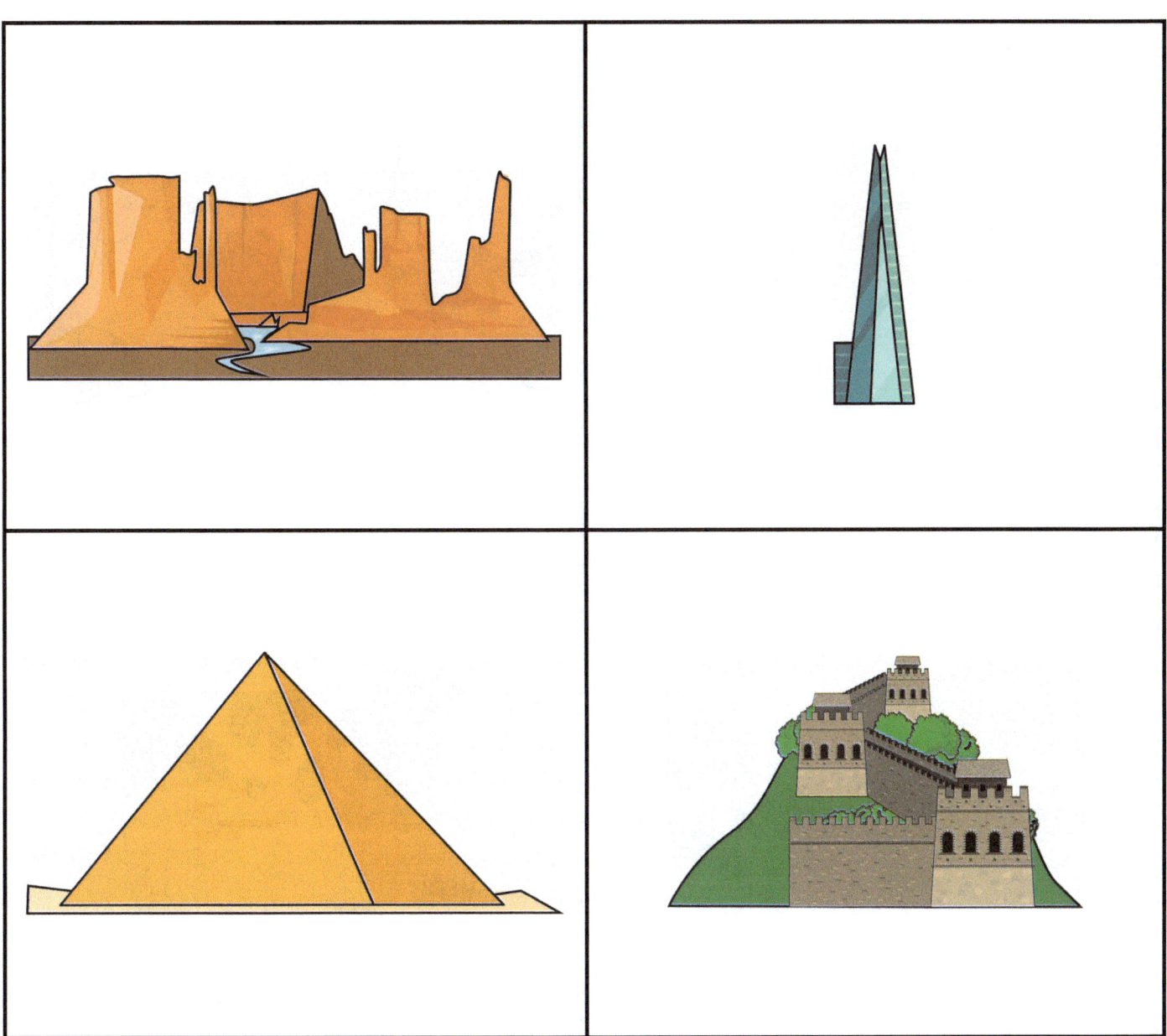

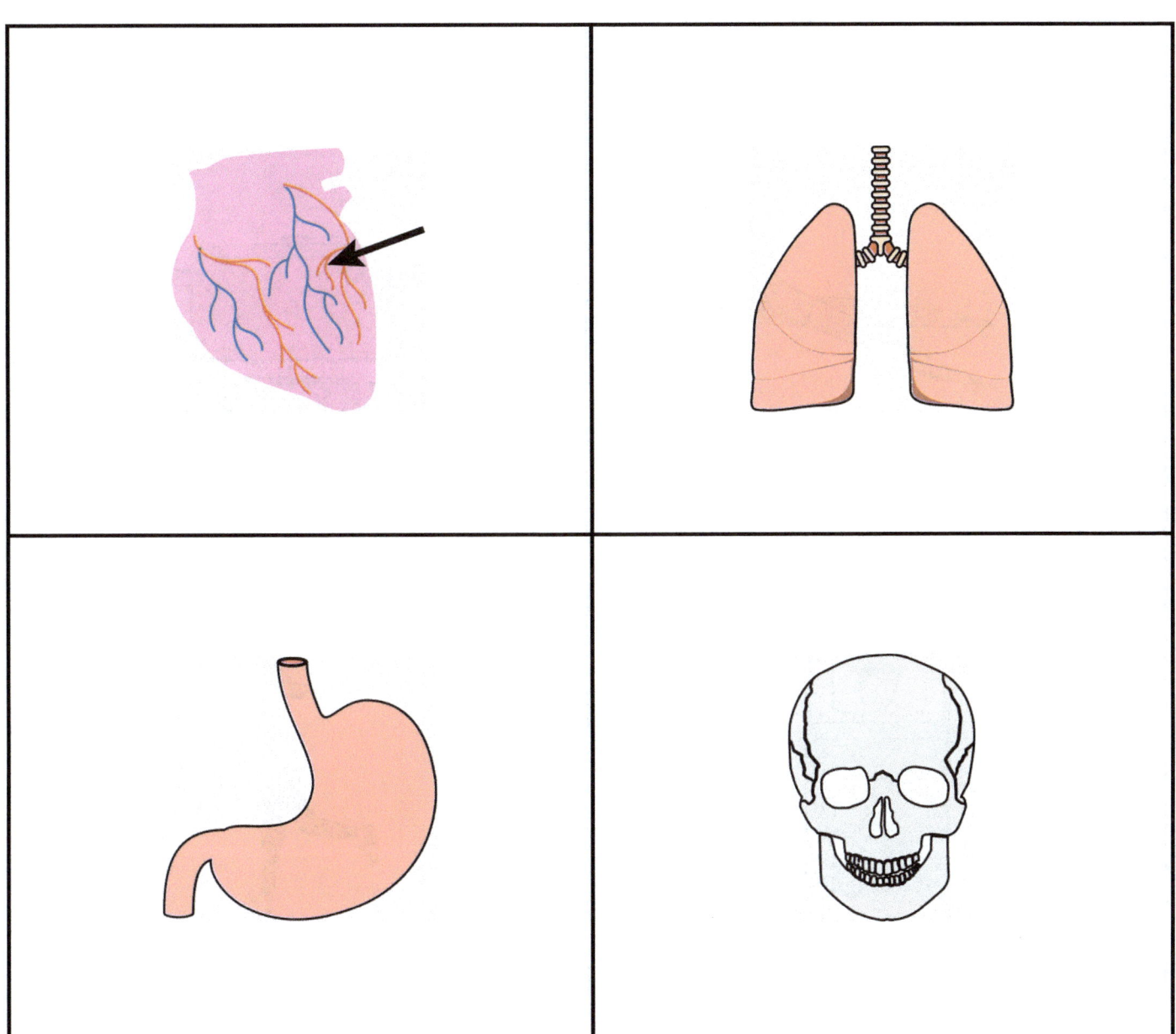

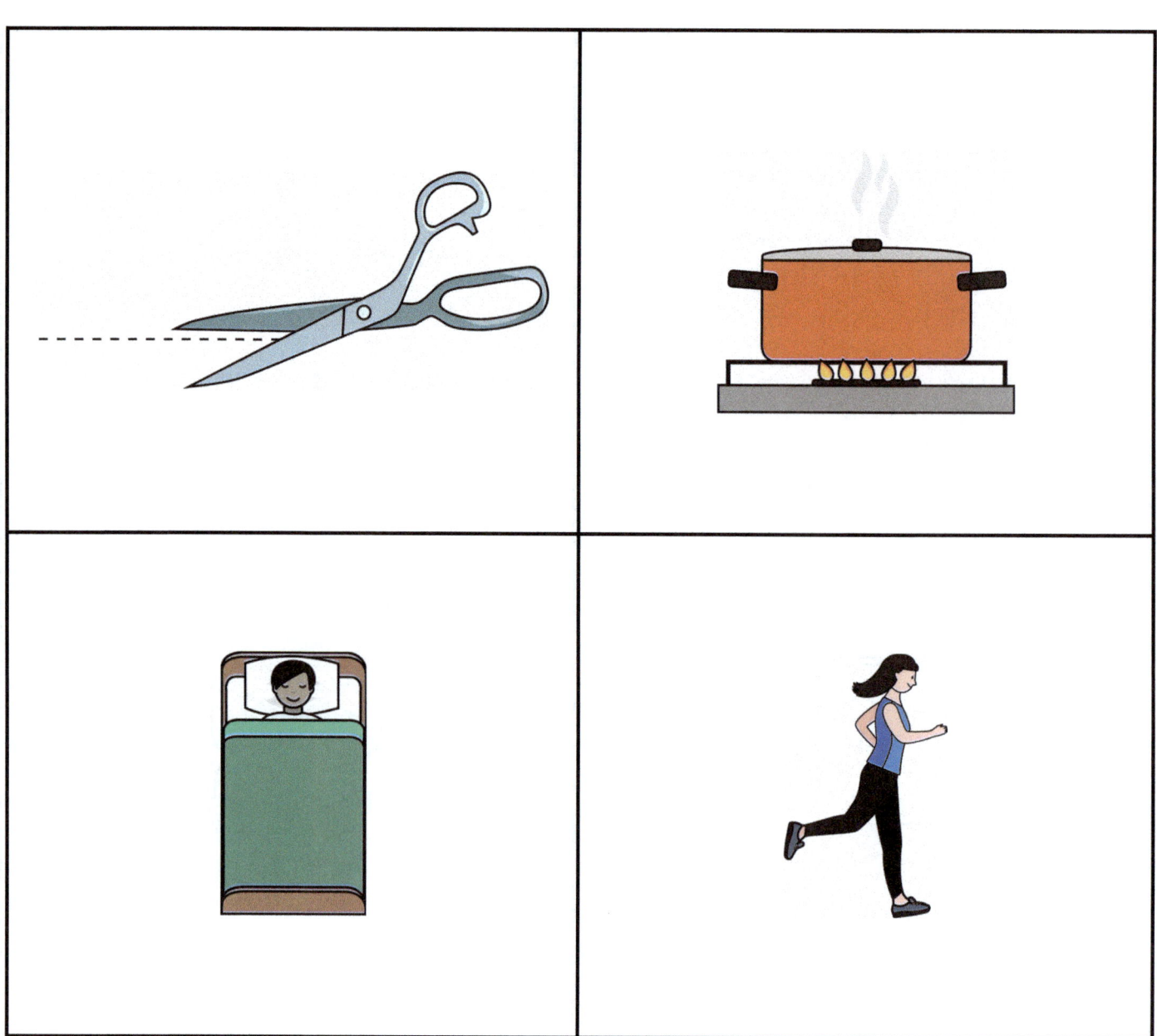

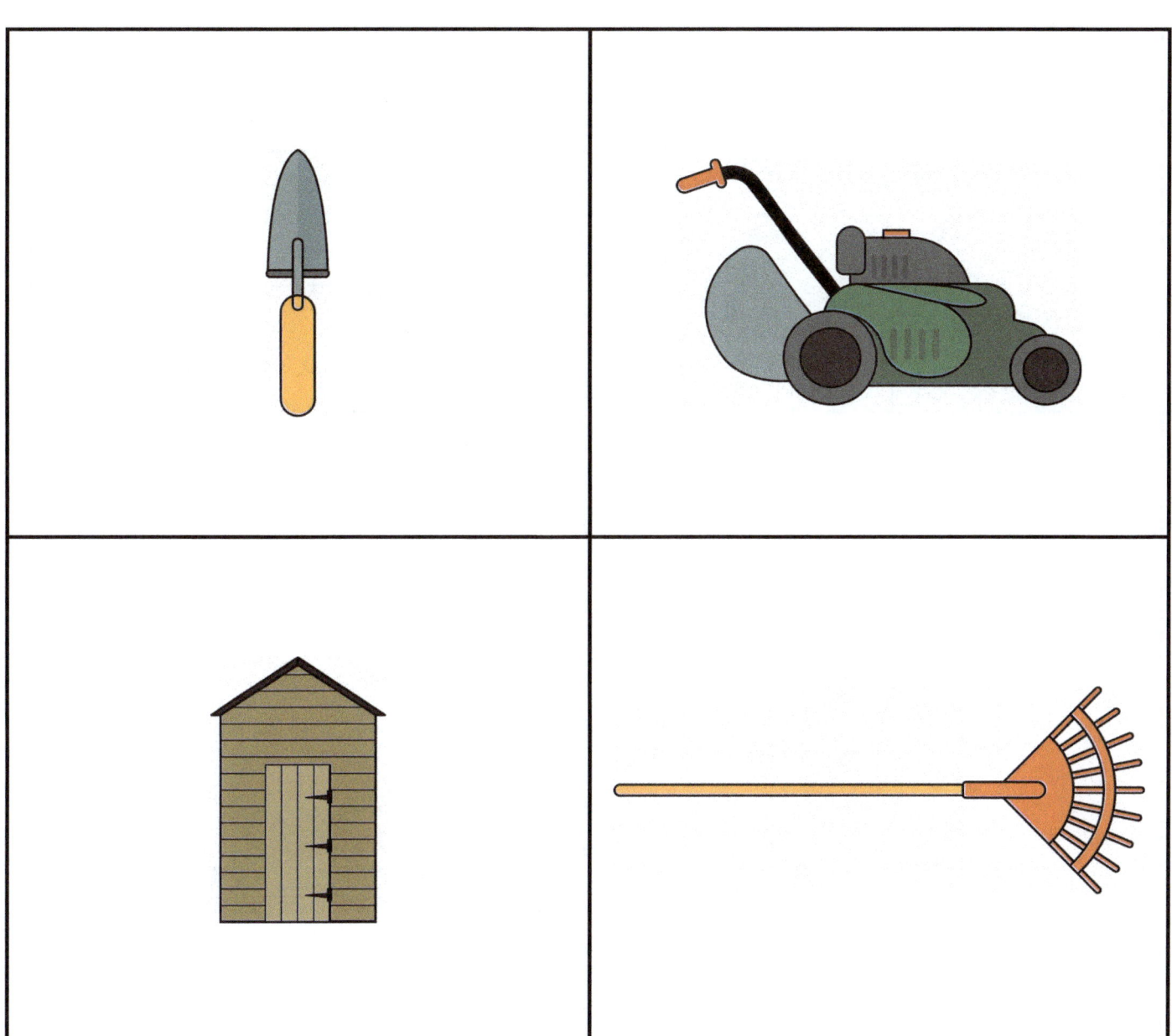

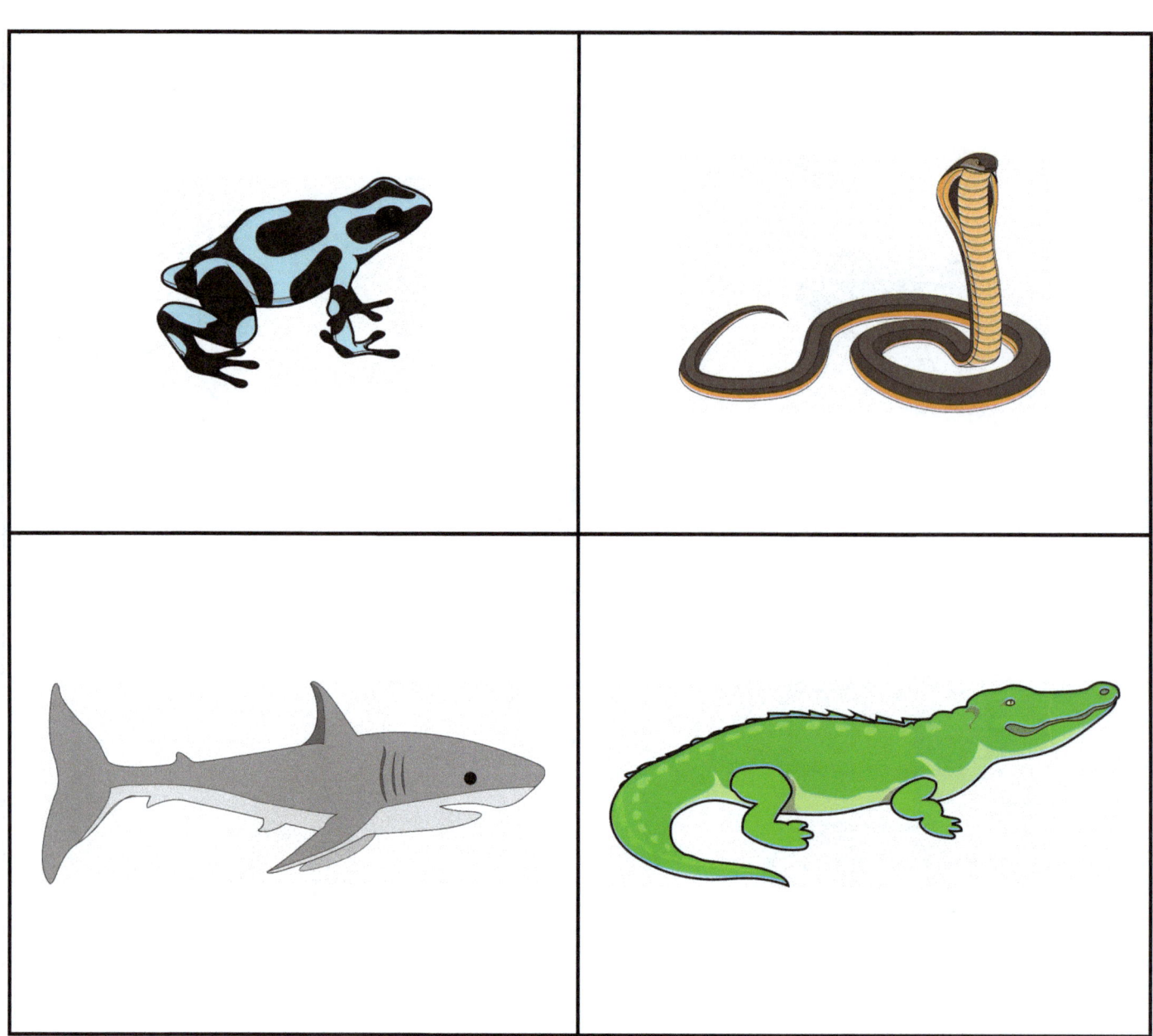

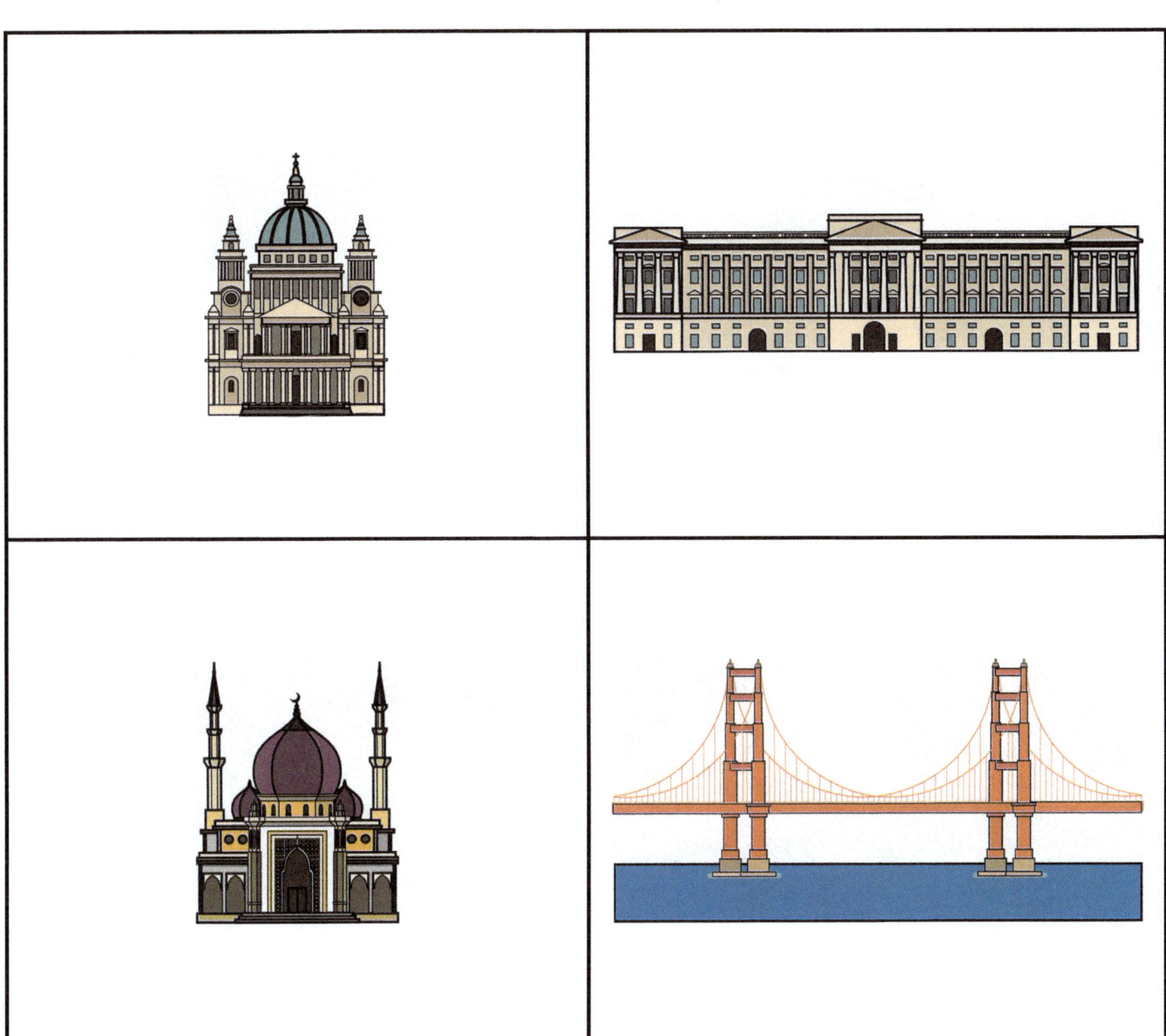

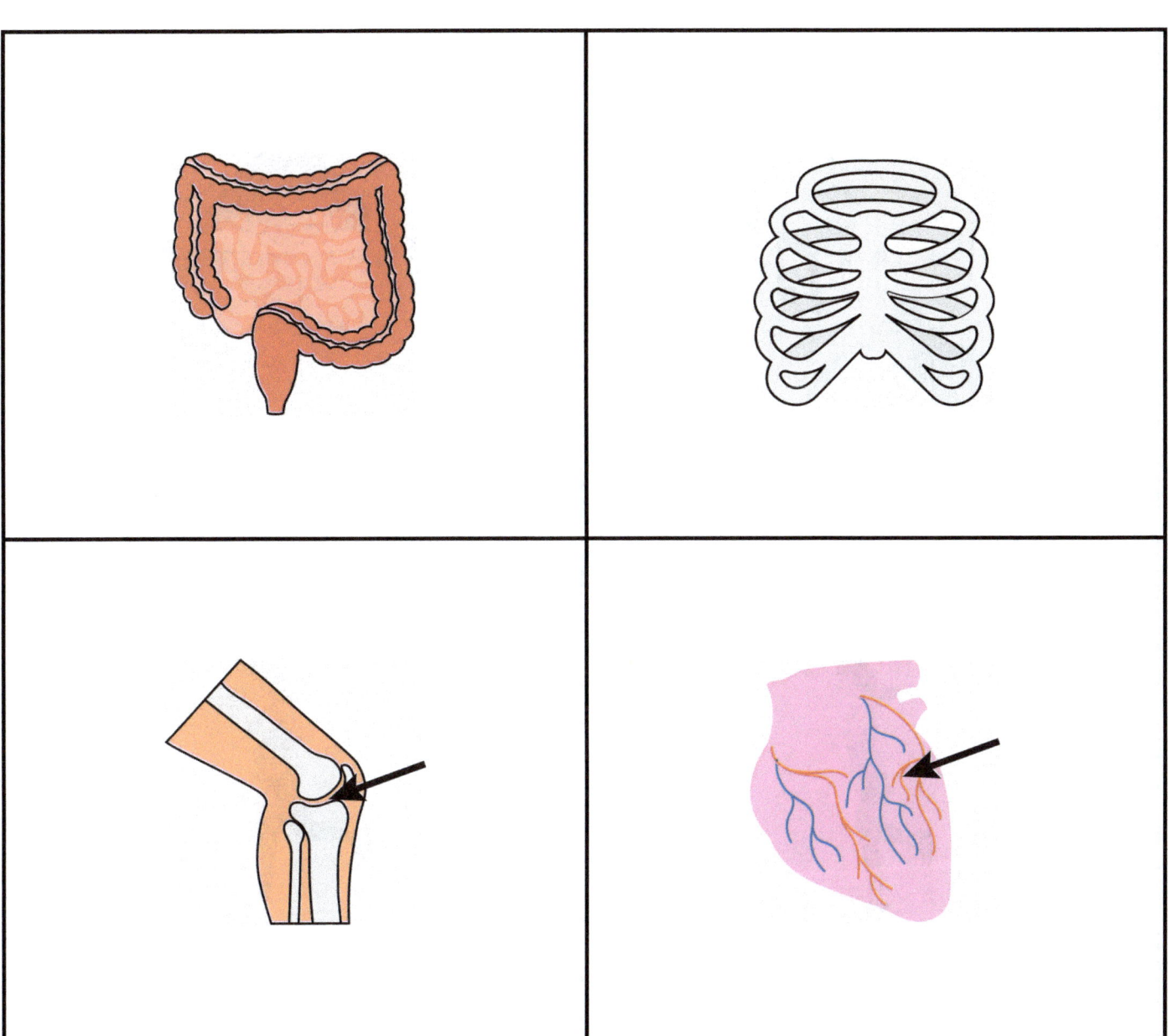

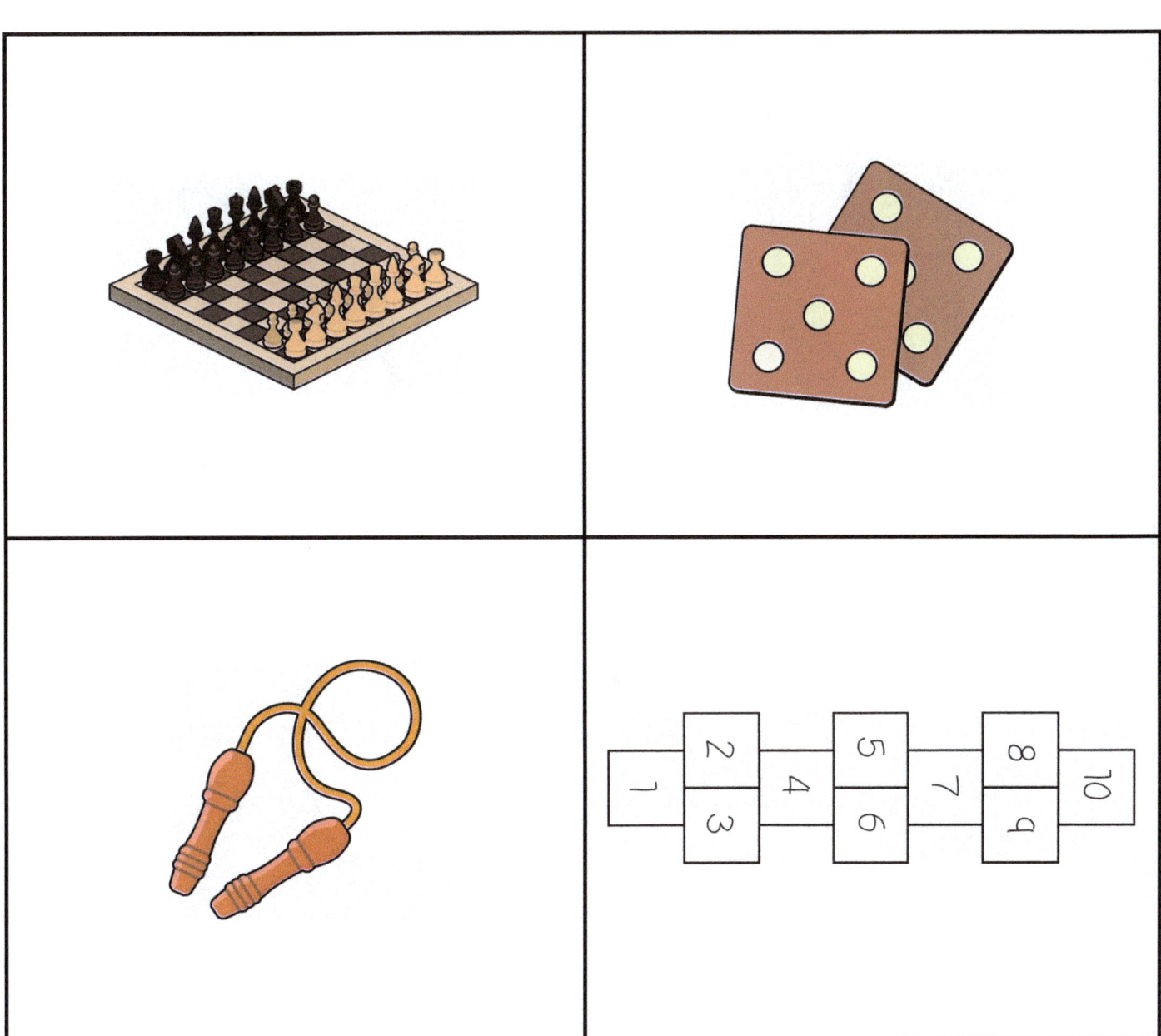

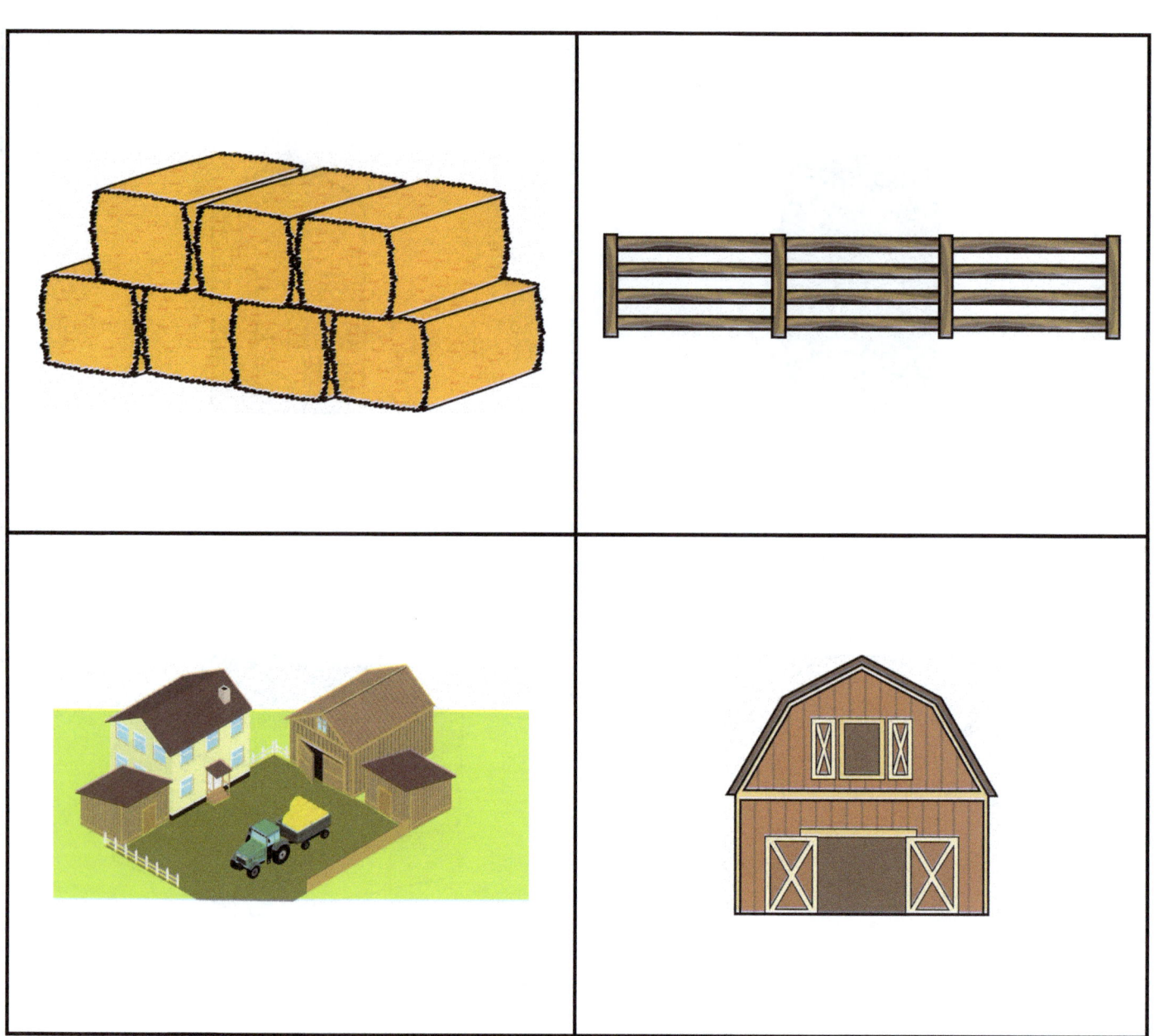

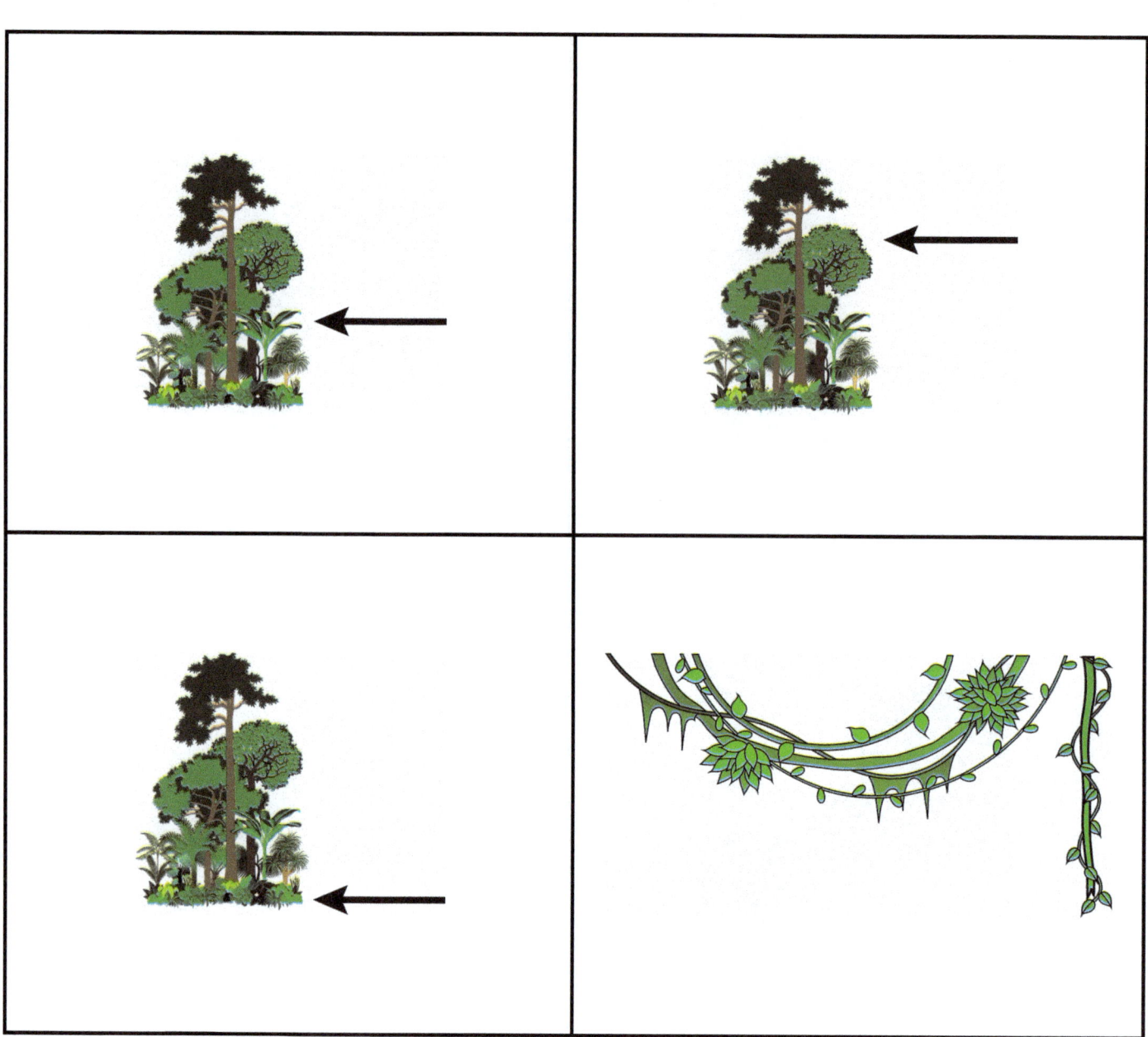

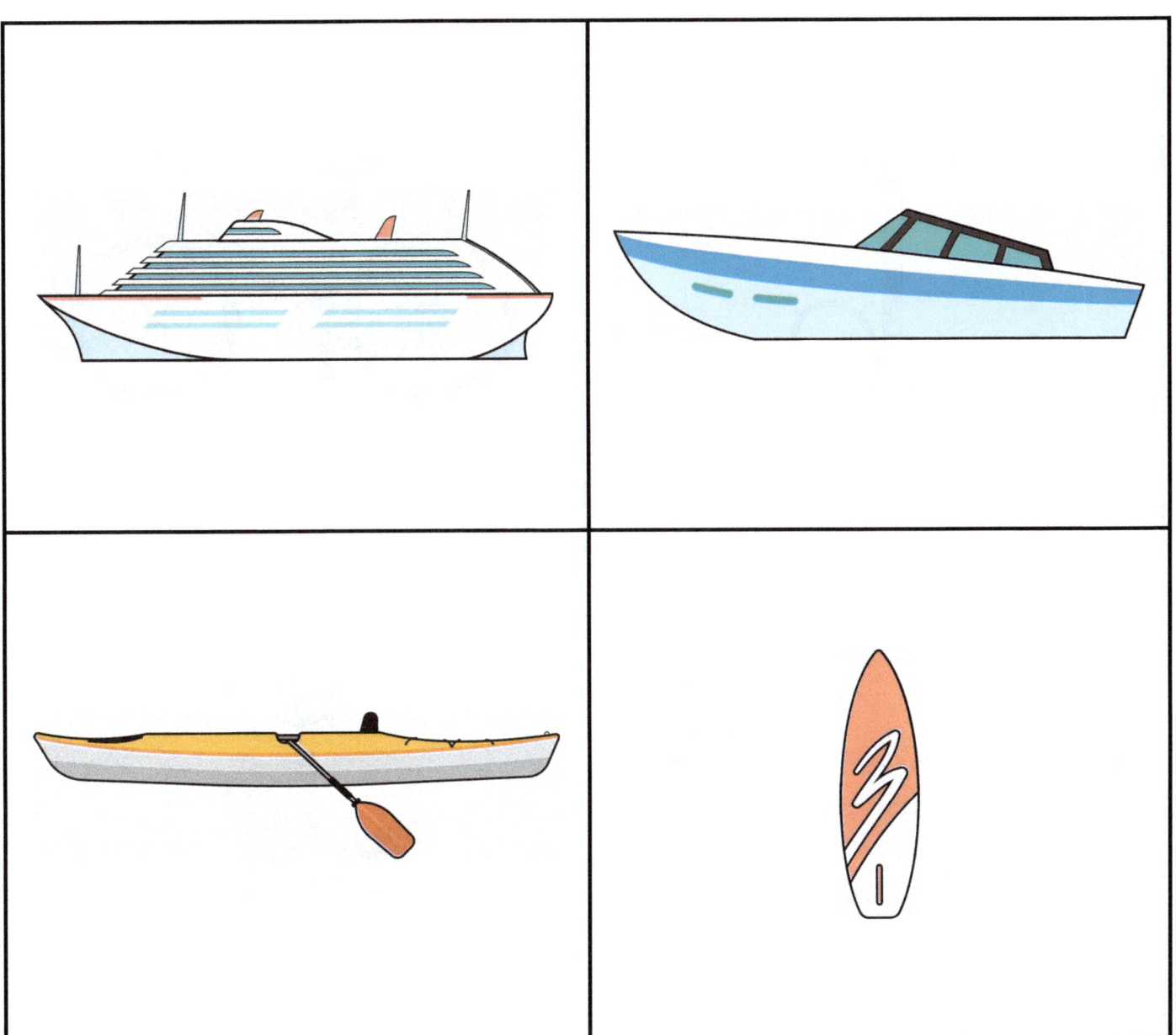

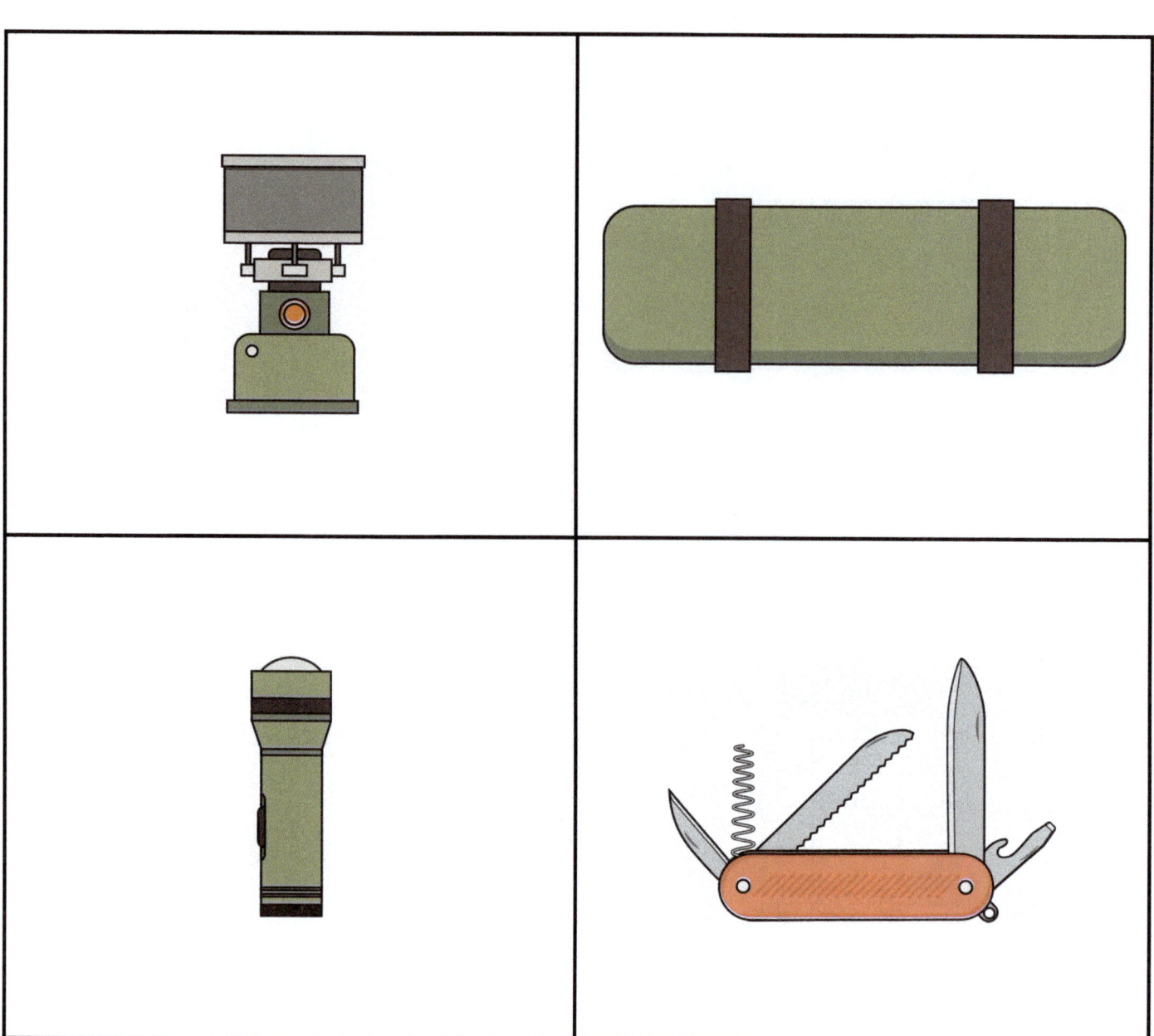

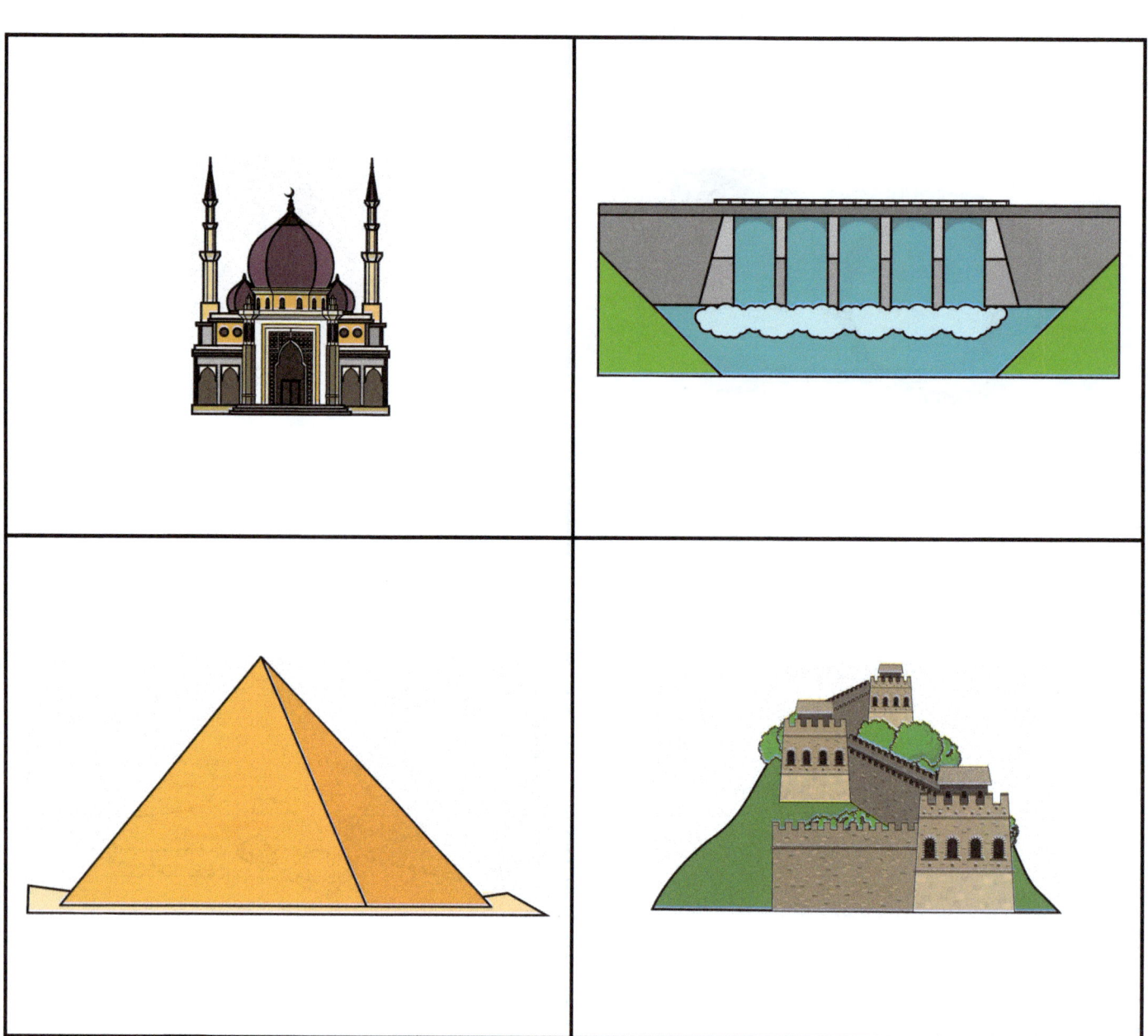

Half termly tests

Half termly test 1

Teacher prompt:
Can you tell me which one shows …? Or
Can you show me the …?

Word tested:
1   heart
2   sewing
3   digging
4   tennis
5   playing cards
6   whiskers
7   egg
8   seeds
9   wheelbarrow
10   stable
11   panda
12   jellyfish
13   hermit crab
14   toucan
15   yacht

Half termly test 2

Teacher prompt:
Can you tell me which one shows …? Or
Can you show me the …?

Word tested:
1   handlebars
2   computer
3   sleeping bag
4   conductor
5   groom
6   axe
7   volcano
8   cauliflower
9   fruit
10   waterproof
11   skyscraper
12   carnivore
13   desert
14   wall
15   herbivore

Half termly tests

Half termly test 3

Teacher prompt:
Can you tell me which one shows …? Or
Can you show me the …?

Word tested:
1   skull
2   sleeping
3   fighting
4   cricket
5   noughts and crosses
6   flipper
7   caterpillar
8   soil
9   rake
10   duck pond
11   kangaroo
12   shark
13   anemone
14   leopard
15   pedalo

Half termly test 4

Teacher prompt:
Can you tell me which one shows …? Or
Can you show me the …?

Word tested:
1   saddle
2   tie
3   camp fire
4   popstar
5   photographer
6   tape measure
7   forest fire
8   aubergine
9   meat
10   transparent
11   canyon
12   reptiles
13   polar regions
14   palace
15   mammals

Half termly tests

Half termly test 5

Teacher prompt:
Can you tell me which one shows …? Or
Can you show me the …?

Word tested:
1   intestines
2   hopping
3   climbing
4   cycling
5   hopscotch
6   tusk
7   frogspawn
8   compost
9   hosepipe
10   haystack
11   camel
12   mosquito
13   starfish
14   vines
15   speedboat

Half termly test 6

Teacher prompt:
Can you tell me which one shows …? Or
Can you show me the …?

Word tested:
1   tyres
2   calculator
3   penknife
4   microphone
5   rings
6   ladder
7   avalanche
8   sweet potato
9   lentils
10   flexible
11   mosque
12   insects
13   coral reef
14   waterfall
15   ocean

Half termly test 1 record sheet

	Word tested	Word correctly identified (✓)
1	heart	
2	sewing	
3	digging	
4	tennis	
5	playing cards	
6	whiskers	
7	egg	
8	seeds	
9	wheelbarrow	
10	stable	
11	panda	
12	jellyfish	
13	hermit crab	
14	toucan	
15	yacht	

Half termly test 2 record sheet

	Word tested	Word correctly identified (✓)
1	handlebars	
2	computer	
3	sleeping bag	
4	conductor	
5	groom	
6	axe	
7	volcano	
8	cauliflower	
9	fruit	
10	waterproof	
11	skyscraper	
12	carnivore	
13	desert	
14	wall	
15	herbivore	

Half termly test 3 record sheet

	Word tested	Word correctly identified (✓)
1	skull	
2	sleeping	
3	fighting	
4	cricket	
5	noughts and crosses	
6	flipper	
7	caterpillar	
8	soil	
9	rake	
10	duck pond	
11	kangaroo	
12	shark	
13	anemone	
14	leopard	
15	pedalo	

Half termly test 4 record sheet

	Word tested	Word correctly identified (✓)
1	saddle	
2	tie	
3	camp fire	
4	popstar	
5	photographer	
6	tape measure	
7	forest fire	
8	aubergine	
9	meat	
10	transparent	
11	canyon	
12	reptiles	
13	polar regions	
14	palace	
15	mammals	

Half termly test 5 record sheet

	Word tested	Word correctly identified (✓)
1	intestines	
2	hopping	
3	climbing	
4	cycling	
5	hopscotch	
6	tusk	
7	frogspawn	
8	compost	
9	hosepipe	
10	haystack	
11	camel	
12	mosquito	
13	starfish	
14	vines	
15	speedboat	

Half termly test 6 record sheet

	Word tested	Word correctly identified (✓)
1	tyres	
2	calculator	
3	penknife	
4	microphone	
5	rings	
6	ladder	
7	avalanche	
8	sweet potato	
9	lentils	
10	flexible	
11	mosque	
12	insects	
13	coral reef	
14	waterfall	
15	ocean	